BAKERSFIELD, CALIFORNIA
JUL 16 1962
CITY SCHOOLS LIBRARY

LONG-AGO STORIES
OF CALIFORNIA

Long-Ago Stories

# of California

by NANCY and JOHN RAMBEAU

Illustrated by SABINA and JEAN YATES

CALIFORNIA STATE SERIES

Published by CALIFORNIA STATE DEPARTMENT OF EDUCATION
Sacramento, 1957

Copyright, 1957, by
HARR WAGNER PUBLISHING COMPANY

printed in
CALIFORNIA STATE PRINTING OFFICE
SACRAMENTO 2ND PRINT, 40M 1958

TO YOUNG AMERICANS

CALIFORNIA! Since long ago, the name has held a kind of magic for men. From the time of Juan Rodríguez Cabrillo, men have come here from many different parts of the world. Some of the early pioneers crossed the seas in sailing ships. Some came on foot or in wagon trains. All of them had to face some kind of danger—mountain snows, burning deserts, savage Indians, or ocean storms. However men came to California in the early days, the journey was one of endless hardship.

The California pioneers came here for many different reasons. Some were looking for land and power. Some wanted new ports for trading ships. Many wanted gold and riches. Still others came in search of new homes and better ways of living.

Yet these people gave to California much more than they took for themselves. They gave of their courage, their hard work, and their ideas. They brought with them their colorful customs and their ways of life. Because of their gifts, California is still a magic place to live in—unlike any other in the world!

The early Californians were people of many races and many faiths. Telling the story of all of them would take many books. *Long-Ago Stories of California* tells of six peoples—Indians, Spaniards, Mexicans, Americans, Chinese, and Italians. Each of these groups played an important part in the history of our state.

Chumash Boy, Tomás, Luisa, Jed and Sally Winters, Yat Sang, and Domenic are some of the young people you will meet in this book. Its stories are fast-moving and will hold your interest to the very end. They paint a picture of six groups of people and of their ways of life—of how they lived and worked and played. Our stories tell of their foods, their clothing, and their homes. They tell of their tools and weapons, and of their ways of making a living. You will be excited by a cattle stampede, a hunt for runaway Indians, and a battle with a shark.

You will learn that men of other times and places have shared a common dream—the dream of a better way of life for themselves and their children. You will see how California grew—out of the dreams and hard work of different peoples. Most important of all, you will learn that our lives are richer today because of the peoples who lived here long ago.

NANCY RAMBEAU
JOHN RAMBEAU

CONTENTS

CHUMASH BOY 3

THE BLACK PEARL OF LA PAZ . . 33

THE MAGIC DOOR 61

GO WEST FOR GOLD! 95

CHINA BOY 121

STRANGER AT CHERRY HILL . . 155

LOOK-UP NAMES 183

LOOK-UP WORDS 185

BOOKS TO READ 191

In Indian Days

THE first Californians came from faraway Asia. No one knows just when or why they came. We do know that they had been in California thousands of years before the Spanish explorers came.

The California Indians were unlike other American Indians. Nature gave them plenty of food and a warm climate. They did not need to build strong houses or plant crops. The Indians of California had little need to fight, so they did not form strong tribes. They did not travel far, or learn new ways of living. They were cut off from the rest of the world by sea and mountains.

Among the California Indians was a group called the Chumash people. They lived near the place we call Santa Barbara. "Chumash Boy" is the story of a young Indian who saw the coming of Juan Rodríguez Cabrillo—a story of California in the year 1542.

CHUMASH BOY

1

Chumash Boy sat in the shadow of the rock, waiting. He had planned his escape well. It was almost time for him to start.

Moonlight lay across the water. The tide was coming in. The boy must wait only a little longer. Behind him, the village was quiet. Smoke rose from the dying fire. A man sat beside the fire.

"He will soon be sleepy," thought Chumash Boy.

The young Indian had been hiding beside the rock for a long time. He had hardly dared to move or breathe. Closer and closer came the water. Now there was only a tiny strip of sand between the water and his hiding place.

Somewhere a dog barked, and another joined in. Chumash Boy looked at the man by the fire. He was asleep. The noise had not wakened him.

It was now or never! The boy slipped from his hiding place. His nets and harpoon were already in his boat. He quickly found the other things he had hidden for his trip. Water, tools, weapons, his robe—all were in his boat. He pushed the boat quietly across the sand. His heart was beating fast.

With one last push, the boat was free. Chumash Boy had no time to waste now. He paddled hard. He did not look back until he was far out on the water.

The boy saw dots of light all along the shore. They were the fires of the Chumash villages that lined the ocean. There, near the river, was Shuku, his home.

Chumash Boy saw the fires of Kolok far away. Enemies of his family lived there. Many moons ago, they had come to his village in the night. They had set fire to his father's house. The fire had burned everything his family owned.

Many of his family had been lost in the fire. Only Chumash Boy and his father had come out alive, and the boy had been badly burned.

The boy's father had been saved because the men did not sleep with their families. Every night they went to the sweat house to smoke and talk. They slept there, with their bows and arrows beside them.

The next day the father had set off for Kolok. But he had never reached his enemies' village. And he had never come back.

Chumash Boy had lived in his uncle's house since that night. His uncle was lazy and evil. He was not a kind man.

The chiefs of Shuku and Kolok had met after the fire. They had decided that the Kolok Indians must pay for what had been burned. The enemies had given many skins, baskets, and strings of shells to Chumash Boy. But his evil uncle had taken all of them. With his father gone, there was no one to get them back for the boy.

"You are too young for these things," the uncle had said. "I will keep them for you."

But the boy had known that his uncle was lying. He had known that his uncle would never give the things to him.

The uncle had also said many things that were not true about Chumash Boy's father. "He did not try to go to Kolok," the uncle had said. "Your father was afraid to fight his enemies. He ran away. He brought shame on our family."

Chumash Boy looked up at the bright stars. "The rest of my family are star people now," he thought. "Someday I will find out what happened to my father. Then I will return and tell my people the truth."

The paddle lay across the boy's knees. Both ends of the paddle were flat and wide. The young Indian held the paddle tightly. It had belonged to his father.

"My father was strong and wise and brave. He did not run away," the boy said to himself. He dipped the paddle into the water, first on one side of the canoe, then on the other. The boat shot forward.

The moon was bright. Across the water, Chumash Boy could see the dark shape of an island. He pushed on. The waves slapped hard against his boat.

He must not let the current carry him too far south. There was one island he must miss. Its people were not Chumash Indians. They spoke a strange tongue and had strange ways. They built their huts of skins and the bones of whales. The people on this island guarded their fishing waters day and night. Any Chumash found in those waters would be killed.

Chumash Boy fought the current with all his might. His arms and back hurt. At last he could fight no longer. He laid the paddle across his knees.

He prayed, "Oh, Spirit of my Father, carry me to a safe place."

Then the boy's head dropped. His eyes closed. The water lapped softly against his boat. He listened for a time and thought, "Surely, I will not drift far." He was soon asleep.

2

The cry of sea birds wakened the runaway boy. He heard the roar of waves—just in time! He was in danger of being thrown against the rocks! He paddled hard. At last he moved his boat away from the rocks and into a small bay.

Chumash Boy jumped into the water. He quickly pulled his boat up onto the sand. But when he looked about him, his heart sank. The current had taken him to the wrong island.

There were no villages on this island. It was very small. It was covered with brush. Chumash Boy knew that fishermen sometimes camped here. But he seemed to be alone on the island now.

The boy looked at the many birds flying high in the air. "There will be plenty of eggs and fish to eat here," he thought. "But what about water?" His water basket was almost empty. He must find more water soon.

An old trail led up from the shore. There was a chance that it led to a spring. The boy had to find out. He climbed the trail. Loose rocks rolled down the hill behind him.

Chumash Boy had not gone far when he found a small hut. There were bones and fish heads everywhere. He saw what was left of a fire. "Some fishermen must have left this," he said to himself. With his foot, he felt the gray ashes.

The ashes were still warm! Someone was on the island.

The boy looked at the ground carefully. He saw the print of a man's foot.

Suddenly, the young Indian felt that he was in danger. He thought of his boat on the beach. Turning, he ran back over the rocks. At one place he fell. At that very moment, a big rock sailed over his head. If he had not fallen, it would have hit him.

At last Chumash Boy reached the beach. He quickly shoved his boat into the water. With a running jump, he was in it. He paddled for his life. All at once, he heard a noise. Turning, he saw an arrow stuck in the side of his boat.

The boy did not stop paddling until he felt that he was safe again. Then he rested a moment. He took a long drink from his nearly empty water basket. The basket was one his grandmother had made long ago. It was woven of grasses. Inside, it was covered with tar to make it watertight.

Chumash Boy looked over the other things in his boat. He had brought only what he would need to keep himself alive. There was a robe made of rabbitskins. It would keep him warm at night. Like the other boys of his tribe, he wore no clothing in summer. But he rubbed mud on his arms and legs when it was cold. And he sometimes wore a fur robe in the winter.

The cooking basket that Chumash Boy had brought along was also lined with tar. He had a large carrying basket with him, too. But his tools were very few. He carried his fire sticks in a net wound around his waist.

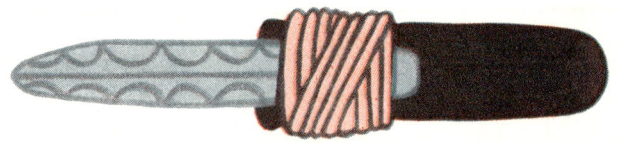

The knife his father had made for him was stuck in his hair. He was especially proud of this knife. Its handle was made of polished wood. Its blade was a hard piece of stone. He sharpened the blade with flint.

Chumash Boy also had a throwing stick in his boat. With this, he could kill rabbits and other small animals. Although he had brought along only a few pine nuts to eat, he had his fine harpoon with him. Perhaps he might even kill a sea lion with it.

Tired though he was, the boy knew that he had been resting long enough. His first job was to catch some fish. It was many hours since he had eaten.

From a small bag, Chumash Boy took some ground

cactus leaves. He put the ground leaves into the water for bait. Then he threw out his net and waited. As he waited, he thought of his fine boat. It took a long time to make such a boat.

The boy's people had gone far up the river to the mountain. The men had hunted through the thick forest for fallen trees. They had split the fallen logs into planks and had carried the rough boards down to the village. They had scraped the planks smooth with

sharp shells, and had made holes in them. Putting strips of leather through the holes, they had then tied the planks together. Finally they had filled every crack and hole with hot tar.

Proud of his boat, Chumash Boy said to himself, "My people make the best boats of all."

He was right. The Chumash people made better boats than any of the other Indians who lived in California.

3

The sun was low in the sky. Chumash Boy ate two of the smaller fish he had caught. He put the other four into his net and closed it. Then he put the net behind his boat to drag along in the water. The boy's mouth was dry, but all his drinking water was gone.

Chumash Boy knew that he must get to the big island before night came. He knew of a village there, called Nimalala. He was sure of a welcome there. Nimalala men had often come to Shuku to trade.

The boy stood up in his boat, looking at the shore. Suddenly, the boat rocked so hard that it nearly upset. Chumash Boy was thrown on his back. His paddle flew out of his hand. Crying with pain, he crawled to the back of the boat. He looked over the edge.

A few bits of net were left. But his four precious fish were gone!

Chumash Boy was angry. He hit his fist against the boat. Then he saw the shark. Its big, wet body and strong teeth shone in the sun. After eating, the boy had thrown the fish heads over the side of his boat. The blood had brought the shark. Chumash Boy thought fast. His paddle was drifting away. He could not swim after it. The shark would kill him. Without the paddle, he would be lost!

There was only one thing to do. The boy grabbed his harpoon. With a great jab, he drove it into the shark's throat. The big fish rolled over. Knife in hand, Chumash Boy dived from the boat. He swam after his paddle.

The shark was fighting for its life. Chumash Boy reached the boat with his paddle. He pulled himself over the side.

The shark was tired. Before long, it was floating, belly up and quite still. Chumash Boy paddled up beside it. This time he would not lose his catch!

The boy tugged and pulled until the wet body was in his boat. The shark was nearly as long as he was.

He dipped the paddle into the dark water and made for the shore. Some children came out to meet him. Their eyes were wide when they saw the shark.

"Your chief was my father's friend," Chumash Boy told them. "Take me to him."

The chief was tall and strong. His robe came down to his feet. It was made of beautiful feathers. The chief looked kindly at Chumash Boy. He saw the boy's many burns. He saw that the boy's hair was cut short. This was the Indian sign that there had been a death in the family.

The chief called to his wife, "Bring water and food." Then he said to Chumash Boy, "Come, my son. You are welcome here."

Chumash Boy entered the chief's house. The chief was the richest man in the village. Even so, his house was poorer than the houses on the mainland. Chumash Boy saw sleeping mats on the floor. At home, his people slept on raised beds.

"I have killed a shark," the boy said. "It is in my boat. You will find pine nuts there, too." He knew that these people had little to eat but fish. He was glad that he had brought the shark and the pine nuts to them.

The chief smiled, then said, "But you must rest now. I will send someone for the things in your boat."

When Chumash Boy had eaten, he told the chief about his family. Then he added in a low voice, "It is said that my father ran away. You knew my father, oh, Chief. Do you believe that?"

"I do not," answered the chief. "I knew your father well." Then he added in a cold voice, "And—I know your uncle!"

Chumash Boy looked into the old man's eyes. Could it be that the chief knew more than he was telling?

Whatever it was, the old man was not yet ready to say more. "If you are rested enough, tell me of your escape," he said to Chumash Boy.

"I planned for many days to leave Shuku," the boy began. "A little at a time, I gathered the things I would need for my trip. I hid them away. But my uncle kept watching my father's boat.

"When the time came to gather the pine nuts and acorns, the people of my village went to the mountain. Only the old men and women stayed behind. My uncle wanted to stay, too. But our chief made him go.

"I went with them. But on the fourth day of the harvest, I slipped away. I made sure that no one saw me. I ran back to our village. It was dark when I reached the river. I waited until the old people of the village were asleep. Then I started across the water."

Then Chumash Boy told the chief what had happened to him on the island. He told of his fight with the shark. The chief sat quietly for a time. Then he said, "It is well that you left Shuku. There is much that I must tell you. But it can wait until morning. Sleep now, my son."

4

Chumash Boy smelled steaming mush. The chief's wife was cooking breakfast. She put hot stones into the cooking basket with some water and acorn meal. Then she added a few pieces of fish. The mush was soon cooked. The woman took the stones out of the basket and left the mush to cool.

The chief spoke. "You must leave here, my son. Your uncle will notice that the boat is gone. He will know that you left by water. He knows that I am your father's friend. He may come here to look for you."

"But why?" the boy asked. "He hates me. Why would he want to take me back to Shuku?"

"Do not forget that your uncle had much to gain by your father's death," the chief said. "You will soon be a man. Then you will ask for what is rightly yours."

"But I won't do that," Chumash Boy cried. "I only want to be away from him."

"He is a man without honor," the chief said. "He lives with fear. If he finds you, you will never get home alive."

The boy was quiet. Could it be that his uncle was a truly evil man?

"Listen. I was told this story," the chief said. "A trading party came to the sea from a village beyond the mountain. On the way home, they found a dying man on the trail. There was a knife wound in his back. The men carried him across the mountain to their village. The chief's daughter took pity on him.

"The man soon grew strong and well. But he had forgotten his name, and where he came from."

Chumash Boy jumped to his feet. "Oh, Chief, that man was my father! I feel sure he was."

"Wait, my son," answered the chief. "We cannot be sure of that yet. But I was told this, too. The man was found on the trail that leads to Kolok. His hair was cut close to his head—the sign of a death in the family."

The boy's eyes burned. "Who told you this?" he asked.

"A messenger from Tukan."

Chumash Boy thought quickly. Tukan was a village on a small island far to the north.

"I must leave at once," he said.

The chief nodded. "Your boat is ready. You will find food for the trip and a new net in it. Let no one see you on your way. My friends at Tukan will help you."

"I cannot find words to thank you, oh, Chief," said Chumash Boy. "I go now."

"Go," the old man said. This was the Indian way of saying good-by.

Chumash Boy set off. He paddled out into the water and stayed far from shore. The sky was clear, but the water was rough.

"The time of strong winds and high waters will be coming soon," he thought.

Later that day, Chumash Boy saw a great whale. It was rolling and diving. The boy was glad when it turned and swam away. No Indian would try to kill a great whale. But one of the huge beasts sometimes swam into shallow water and died there. Then the Indians used its bones to make tools.

Chumash Boy paddled all night long. He could not lose time sleeping. Black clouds sailed across the moon. The wind rose. Then he heard the roll of thunder. The boy fought the storm all night. But the sky was clear again when morning came. At last he could see the island where Tukan was. He knew that his journey was almost over.

In the harbor at last, Chumash Boy saw a strange sight—two ships with tall, white wings. The boy moved closer. Was this a war party from some faraway tribe? Would he find the messenger at Tukan dead or alive? His heart beat fast as he paddled for the shore.

5

Chumash Boy ran through Tukan. All the Indians there were busy. If they were making ready for war, he saw no signs of it.

The chief spoke to the boy kindly. "Good. You have come in time for our feast. We have other visitors, too."

"I saw the tall boats," said Chumash Boy.

"These men come from far away," the chief told him. "They speak a strange tongue. They have strange ways. But they are friendly."

Then the chief smiled. "That is enough about the men for now," he said. "I know that you want news of your father."

"Yes, yes," the boy cried.

A young Indian entered the chief's house. He was the messenger Chumash Boy was seeking. He told Chumash Boy the same story that the first chief had told him.

"Take me to the village beyond the mountain," begged Chumash Boy. "Let me see my father. Then perhaps he will remember."

The chief shook his head. "Your uncle might follow. Your father's life would be in danger. No, you must stay here. We have a better plan."

The messenger said, "I will bring your father from the mountains. I will take him to Nimalala. Later, you will meet us there. The chief of Nimalala and a party of his people will take you back to Shuku."

Chumash Boy did not want to stay behind. But he knew that this plan was safer. He pulled the knife from his hair.

"Take this with you," he said. "My father made it. When he sees it, he may remember."

The messenger took the knife. "I go now," he said.

"Go," spoke the chief.

Chumash Boy walked to the beach with the messenger. "You risk much for me," the boy said.

"It is nothing," said the young Indian. "You would do the same for me."

The messenger's boat was soon out on the black water and out of sight. The boy turned, his heart filled with shame.

"I am a coward," he said to himself. "I ran away from home. I would not fight for what was mine. I did no evil. But I let another man do evil. That is just as wrong."

But the boy's mind was made up now. He would go back to Shuku. He would see to it that wrong was made right. As he went back over the trail to Tukan, he felt strong and good inside.

The singing and dancing at Tukan lasted far into the night. The strange men came to the feast. They brought gifts of beads and cloth for all the Indians.

Many of the white men were weak and sick. Their leader had hurt his arm. Chumash Boy noticed that they did not eat any of the Indians' raw fish. He saw their strange knives. They were not made of wood or stone or shell. The blades were hard and bright.

"I do not know why they came here," Chumash Boy said to himself. "But it is a sign from the Spirits. I feel it in my heart. My people have kept the land as it was in the beginning. But these men—they will bring a change."

When the storm was over, it was time for the strange

men to leave. Chumash Boy helped carry wood and water to their ships. At last they set off across the water. The tall, white wings of their ships filled with wind. They were soon out of sight.

Chumash Boy thought of the strange men many times. They had been kind and friendly. But still he was uneasy.

The days passed slowly. Chumash Boy waited for the messenger. Would the man never come?

Chumash Boy did what he could to help his friends in Tukan. He helped to build a house. Long poles were placed in a circle. They were tied together at the top. Grass mats were tied onto the frame. The women dug a wide pit in the middle of the house. They carried the dirt outside and put it against the walls. Then they smoothed the floor. The house had two doors and a smoke hole at the top. There was a shelf of earth all around the inside.

When the house was finished, a family moved into their new home. They held a feast. All the Indians in the village came. They ran races and played games. They sang and danced far into the night.

Chumash Boy waited and waited for the messenger to come back. But there was still no word of his father. Then one day, he at last heard a shout from the beach. He ran down the trail to the water's edge. His heart was beating fast.

6

When Chumash Boy looked out over the bay, his heart sank. He did not see the messenger's boat. Instead, he saw the tall, white wings again.

"Why do the white men come back?" Chumash Boy asked himself.

He soon found out. Their ships needed to be repaired. And their leader was very sick. The brave man was dying.

The people of Tukan were glad to help the white men. Once again, they took wood and water to the white men's ships. They helped to repair them. An Indian law said that every Indian must care for all those in need of help.

The moon of strong winds was almost over. Then one day, a party of white men came from their ships. Their faces were sad. They carried the body of their leader. They made a grave for him on the island and marked it with a cross. Chumash Boy could not read the words on the wooden cross. They would have told him that the dead leader was Juan Rodríguez Cabrillo. Soon afterward, the tall ships sailed away.

One day the chief called for Chumash Boy. "I have news for you," the old man said. "You must go now. Your father is at Nimalala."

Chumash Boy fell on his knees before the chief. "I do not know how to thank you," he said.

"You are always welcome here, my son. Remember that, but go now," the chief told him.

Chumash Boy said good-by to his friends. He quickly made his boat ready. As he left the bay, he looked back at the wooden cross. He thought of the white men, with their strong ships and strange tools.

"They have left their mark upon our land," he said to himself. "One day, they will come again. What will become of my people?"

But these thoughts were soon forgotten. His feeling of sadness left the boy. He would soon be with his father again.

Much later, Nimalala came into sight. Here, at last, was the moment he had waited for.

"My son, my son!" his father cried.

After the joyful greetings were over, there was much work to be done. First, the chief sent a mes-

senger to Shuku. He was to say that a trading party was coming from the island. But he was not to say anything about Chumash Boy and his father. He was not even to mention their names.

A few days later, the party set out. There were many boats and many men in the party. Chumash Boy and his father were among them.

The boy said to his father, "I want to see Uncle's face when he finds that you are alive."

The boy's father smiled and said, "It will not be long now. Look! The people of Shuku are waiting by the water to welcome us."

Chumash Boy and his father jumped from their boat. Together, they walked up behind the uncle. The father placed a hand on the uncle's arm. The evil man turned. His eyes grew wide.

"Brother, are you not happy to see me?" asked the father.

The evil man could not speak. He tried to pull away, but his brother held on to his arm.

"Come," said Chumash Boy's father. "Let us find our chief. We have much to tell him."

The chief looked first at Chumash Boy and then at his father.

"How is this?" he asked. "We thought that you were dead these many moons."

"Ask this one," the father said in a cold voice. He

threw his brother to the ground. The man lay there, shaking with fear.

The boy's father spoke to the chief. "Many moons ago, I set off for our enemies' village. On the way, someone stuck a knife into my back. He left me, thinking that I was dead. It was this man—my own brother.

"I was found by a trading party," Chumash Boy's father went on. "They took me to their village, where I stayed for many moons. The people of Nimalala and Tukan helped my son to find me."

The chief raised his hand. "Wait," he said, turning to the father. "Do you have proof that the man who struck you was your brother?"

The father held out a bone ring. "I made this for my brother when we were boys," he said. "He always wore it. But it slipped from his hand when he tried to kill me."

The uncle began to crawl away, looking at the ring. The other Indians began to whisper to one another. Chumash Boy knew that all of them believed what his father had said.

The chief said angrily to the uncle, "You bring shame on your family, and on our village. Go at once! Never return to Shuku!"

Then the chief turned to Chumash Boy and his father. "Welcome home," he said. "Tomorrow we'll start work on your new house. But tonight—we shall feast and dance!"

The boy walked proudly beside his father up the trail. At last his long journey was ended.

When Mission Bells Rang

AFTER Cabrillo's visit, California was forgotten for two hundred years. In other parts of the world, kings were fighting for power over the seas. At last the Spanish King remembered California—the land Cabrillo had claimed for Spain.

The King knew that England and Russia were looking for new ports. He was afraid of losing California to another country. So he sent more explorers to California. He sent priests to build missions. Families came from Mexico to build the first tiny pueblos.

"The Black Pearl of La Paz" is a story of the early years when California belonged to Spain. It is about a young adventurer named Tomás, who came to California in 1795. By then only thirteen of the missions had been built. California was a wild and lonely place to live in—but an exciting one for Tomás.

THE BLACK PEARL OF LA PAZ

1

Tomás saw a strange man running toward him. The man's pistols, dusty clothing, and the pack of letters he carried told his story. He was the Spanish King's mail carrier. Tomás knew that he was in for trouble.

"Be quick, friend," the man called. "I must have your mule, in the name of the King of Spain."

With an angry look, Tomás jumped from Josefa's back. What was the use of talking? The King's mail carrier was an important man in the Californias. Once a month, he rode between Monterey and Loreto. He never left the trail. He rode day and night without stopping. A fresh horse was waiting for him at every mission. If his horse fell, or was hurt, he took the first animal he saw.

The man threw his pack across Josefa's back. As the man rode off, Tomás shook his fist after him.

"Take care of my mule," the boy called, "or I will have your ears—King, or no King!"

There was no one to hear the boy's angry words. He was alone on the King's Highway. Now, what to do? Tomás wanted to go north. The mail carrier was headed south.

The boy thought a moment. "He'll leave Josefa at the last mission. If I go back for her, I'll have to walk all night. No, it is better to go on. I can get to the next mission before dark."

The sun was hot. The hills were dry and brown. It was lonely without the little mule. For many years, she had been a good friend. In all the world, there were just two things Tomás cared about—only Josefa and his black pearl.

Tomás took the pearl from his belt. It felt cool and smooth in his hand. It was not really black. It was silvery gray, like a winter's moon. He had seen many pearls, but never one so beautiful as his.

"They will never take *this* from me," he said aloud. "Neither the King of Spain nor anyone else."

Tomás had been born in La Paz, a town in Lower California. There were many poor people in La Paz.

Tomás was always the poorest. When he was small, he had often gone hungry. Then one day, he had saved the life of a pearl diver. In return, the man had given him this pearl.

After that, nothing else had ever mattered. The world might think Tomás a beggar. He might be without friends or family. But, with his pearl, he felt rich and important.

Tomás walked on and on. The King's Highway led him over the hills and into a valley. He began to see sheep and cattle in the fields. At last he saw the adobe walls of the mission ahead.

Hearing a voice, Tomás turned. He saw an Indian boy driving oxen in from the fields. The boy waved.

"Wait," he called. "I will walk with you."

The boy was a little younger than Tomás. His long black hair reached to his shoulders. He wore a loose-fitting woolen shirt and woolen pants. A small wooden cross hung from a strip of hide about his neck.

The two boys walked along together. All around them stretched newly plowed fields. They passed gardens and grapevines. Near the mission walls were Indian huts. A few children were playing about. The boys passed the adobe buildings where the mission soldiers lived.

"How is it that you speak Spanish?" Tomás asked in surprise. "Are you not Indian?"

"Yes, I am Indian. I was left at the mission when I was a baby. I have always lived here. I learned Spanish from Father Salazar. My name is Rosario," the boy told him.

"I have come all the way from La Paz," Tomás said. "Part of the way, I worked as a mule driver."

The trip had not been fun. But Tomás made it sound exciting.

"You are a long way from your home," Rosario said, smiling.

"Ha! I cannot get far enough away," Tomás said. "I am never going back. I am going to see the world —all of it."

The boys came to a pile of adobe bricks. Tomás kicked one of them with his toe.

"Here in Upper California, the missions are made of mud," he said. "Where I come from, we have fine churches built of stone." He wanted to brag to this boy. He could not understand why.

The Indian said no more until they came to the gate. Then he said, "I must care for the animals before I eat. You must be tired and hungry. Go to Father Salazar. He will see that you are fed. I'd like to show you our mission tomorrow."

"I hope I'll be gone from here by tomorrow. I must go back for my mule," Tomás said.

"You are not staying?" Rosario asked in surprise.

"Why should I stay?" asked Tomás. "Why do you stare at me?"

"I am sorry," said Rosario. "Do not be angry. There is trouble here at the mission—bad trouble. Father Salazar needs help. All day I have wished for something good to happen. I have prayed for a miracle. When I saw you, I thought—."

Tomás stopped him. "Do not think such things. I bring no miracle. I have troubles of my own."

Rosario sighed. "Goodnight then," he said sadly. He walked away after his animals.

Tomás looked after him. He said to himself, "Make your own miracles, foolish one. I want nothing to do with this hornet's nest."

2

Tomás did not see Father Salazar at first. The mission patio was a busy, noisy place. It was suppertime. Some of the Indians were carrying food to their huts. Ducks, chickens, and geese were pecking about in the dirt. The kitchen was at one end of the patio. It was built like a shed, with a grass roof. An Indian woman there was dipping mush from a large iron pot. Tomás waited his turn behind the Indians. He was soon given a bowlful of hot mush.

After supper, the women went away. The young girls went to their room in the mission. Those with families went to their family huts. The men and boys stayed near the kitchen to say their prayers.

As the singing began, Tomás felt a hand on his arm. It was Rosario's hand.

"There is our Father Salazar. What do you think of him?" he asked.

Tomás turned. His eyes grew wide. "What a giant of a man! He must eat nothing but bull meat," he said. "Surely, such a man has no need for miracles."

"Everyone needs help sometimes," Rosario said quietly.

After the singing, Father Salazar came up to Tomás.

"I am sorry that I could not welcome you sooner," he said. "Father Ávila, my helper, is at one of the rancherias. I have been busier than ever the past few days."

"I lent my mule to the King's mail carrier," explained Tomás. "I must go back for her soon. She will be very unhappy. Do you think I could borrow a horse from you?"

Father Salazar sighed. "It is a bad time for us," he said. "The carrier took one of our horses, too. Father

Ávila and our soldiers have the others. I have only one old mare left."

"Then I must wait for Father Ávila—or walk?" asked Tomás.

"Do not think of walking," Rosario said quickly. "Wait here. There is room."

"The mail carrier brought us all bad news," the priest said. "As you know, Spain and France are at war. Our King has asked for money from the missions. I have none to give." He shook his head sadly. "It is hard to say no. Our country needs help."

Tomás nodded politely. But he was thinking, "The King will get nothing from me! It is all because of him that I am stuck here. Trouble, trouble, trouble! Now I will hear it morning, noon, and night."

Father Salazar turned to Rosario. "There is a bed in the storeroom. Will you take Tomás there? See that he has water and blankets."

Tomás thanked Father Salazar. Rosario gave the visitor a jug of water and a basin to carry. He gave him a bar of hard yellow soap. Rosario himself carried a blanket that had been woven at the mission. He stopped at the kitchen fire to light a candle for his guest.

Tomás looked about him. The room was large and dim. The candle threw long shadows across the dirt floor. Sacks of grain were piled about the walls. In one

corner stood a narrow bed. It was a wooden frame covered with hides.

Rosario put the blanket down and turned to leave.

"Wait," Tomás said. "Tell me a little about this Father Salazar. He could be a rich and important person. Why does he choose to come here?"

"Because he loves us," said Rosario, smiling. "Because he wishes to save our souls. You do not understand that, do you?"

Tomás kicked off his sandals. He rubbed his sore

feet. "You talked of trouble here. What trouble is there?" he asked.

"Oh—many things are wrong," Rosario said slowly. "It has been a dry year. The crops were poor. And the King! The King wants many things done. He is far away. He does not understand how it is here. He wants money. He wants Father Salazar to start a school. He wants all the Indians to learn Spanish—even to read and write it."

Tomás looked at the Indian boy. "You are hiding something, Rosario. Tell me the real trouble!"

A look of fear came over the Indian boy's face. "It is the Spanish soldiers," he said in a low voice. "Some of them are bad. The Indians do not like them. Some of my people even talk of running away. But for Father Salazar, many of them would have left long ago."

"And, if they do run away—what happens?" asked Tomás.

"If an Indian does not belong to the church, he is free to go. But if he belongs to the church, he must stay. He cannot go back to his old way of life. If he leaves, the soldiers will follow him. There will be fighting. It will break Father Salazar's heart," Rosario said sadly.

"Father Ávila is gone. Most of the soldiers are with him," Tomás said slowly. "If any of the Indians are going to run away, this would be a good time, wouldn't it?"

Just then the large mission bell began to ring.

"There is the Bell of the Poor Souls," Rosario said. "I must go to prayers. Give me your suit. I will give it to the women to wash for you."

Tomás looked down at his cotton shirt and pants. They were dusty and dirty from his long walk. He quickly took them off and gave them to Rosario.

Tomás was left alone. He washed himself with water from the jug. It was good to be clean again! He lay down under the blanket. Through the high window he could see the stars. Sounds of music and dancing came from the patio.

Tomás thought of the giant priest and the strange Indian boy. He was almost asleep. Then suddenly he sat up. *The black pearl!*

"Oh, I am a fool! A fool!" he cried.

Tomás had left his pearl in his clothing. He must have his suit back again. He ran to the door and pulled it open. But the patio was dark and quiet now. Only a few chickens roosted in the trees. He could not waken the whole mission looking for Rosario.

Tomás groaned. He closed the door again and went back to bed.

"What a day!" he said angrily. "First my Josefa— now the pearl. I wish I had never left La Paz!"

43

3

Someone was knocking on the door. Tomás rubbed his eyes. Light was coming through the high window.

"It is Rosario with the clothing," Tomás said to himself. "If that pearl is gone,—"

The boy got up, pulled the blanket around him, and opened the door. It was not Rosario who stood there. It was Father Salazar. His face was pale.

"I must find Rosario. Is he with you?" he asked.

"With *me?* If he were here, I would shake him," Tomás said angrily. "He left me with nothing to wear. He has my clothing. My pearl is fastened to my belt."

Father Salazar rubbed a hand over his eyes. "Let me sit down, Tomás. I do not understand about this pearl. Do you mean that Rosario *stole* it?"

"No, no," Tomás groaned. "I left it in my clothing. He did not even know that it was there. But I must get my suit back before it is washed."

"I am very sorry, Tomás," said Father Salazar. "Last night some of the Indians ran away from the mission. I cannot find Rosario. I am afraid that he is with them." The big priest put his head in his hands. "Of all the Indians, there was none I trusted more than Rosario," he said sadly. "Why did he leave us? *Why?*"

Tomás looked at the sad giant. He even forgot about his pearl. He was thinking of a story he had once heard. It was about a priest who started a mission in Lower California. The land was very dry. There was no grass for the mission's cattle. Every day the priest drove the cattle many miles in search of grass. There was not even water for a garden. Even so, the priest planted a garden. He carried water on his back to keep the plants alive. One day he sent Indians to bring greens for the church. They did not understand him. By mistake, they pulled up every plant in his garden.

Tomás thought, "That man must have looked as Father Salazar looks now." Then he said, "But Rosario was happy here. He will come back."

"The others will not let him come back alive," Father Salazar said. "There is nothing to do but wait until Father Ávila returns. Then I will send out the soldiers."

"No, no! Do not send soldiers after Rosario!" Tomás cried. Then he stopped. Why should he care whether the soldiers hurt Rosario? But suddenly he did care. "We cannot wait," he said. "Rosario's life may be in danger. Give me the old mare, and some clothing to wear. I will go for him myself."

Father Salazar looked at Tomás a long time. *"Can I trust this boy?"* his eyes seemed to ask. Then he picked up a stick. He made a map on the dirt floor of the room.

"Here is the rancheria where Father Ávila is," the priest said. "There are other rancherias here, here—and here. To the south, there is a rancho belonging to Don Solá. Find Rosario. He will tell us where the others are."

"Do not worry, I will find him," Tomás said. "This is the only way I will ever get back my pearl."

Before the bell rang for morning prayers, Tomás was on his way. The priest had given him fruit and cheese to take along. He wore some woolen clothing that had been made at the mission.

"I will follow the King's Highway to the rancho," he said to himself. "They will go there first for horses."

The Indians had left on foot. But they had a good start, and they knew the short cuts. This was strange land to Tomás. He dared not cut across the hills. He had to follow the King's Highway. After an hour's hard ride, he came to a big oak tree. Here was the turnoff to the rancho. All at once, the mare stopped so suddenly that Tomás almost fell off her back.

There, lying face down on the trail, was an Indian. Tomás jumped off the mare and bent over the man. The Indian wore mission clothing. There was a bullet in his back!

Tomás moved the Indian into the shade. He gave the injured man a drink of water. Then he put his water bag into the Indian's hand.

"I will be back as soon as I can," he said.

The Indian opened his eyes. He was very weak. But there was nothing more Tomás could do for him then. He knew that he had no time to lose.

Tomás jumped on the mare's back again, and was soon riding hard. At last he saw a corral ahead. Some

Indians were working nearby. They were making adobe bricks. They were going to build a large ranch house. Tomás rode up to a small adobe building. A yellow dog ran out, barking. Don Solá came through the doorway. He carried a gun in his hands.

"I come from the mission," Tomás told him. "I am looking for runaway Indians."

"Yes, I know all about them," Don Solá said angrily. "They have taken my best horses. They have gone to the hills."

"Not all of them, Señor," Tomás said. "One is back on the trail. He has a bullet in his back."

"The others will be dead, too, if I find them," Don Solá said. "I'll teach them to come here and steal."

"Do you mind if I ride over your land?" Tomás asked. "I'd like to find their trail."

Don Solá did not look as though he liked the idea. "Well—go ahead, if you must," he said slowly.

There was an open door behind Don Solá. Tomás saw someone standing just inside. It was an Indian woman. She did not make a sound. But, behind Don Solá's back, she held up something for Tomás to see. It was a small wooden cross on a strip of hide. It was Rosario's cross!

"The boy is still here," Tomás said, under his breath. But how was Tomás to get past the angry Don Solá to find him?

4

The Indian woman moved away without making a sound. Tomás could not let Don Solá know that he had seen her. Then he had an idea!

"I have had a hard ride, Señor," he said. "Could you let me have a little water, please?"

"Yes," said Don Solá. "María will give you some."

Don Solá called, and the woman returned. Tomás followed her inside the house.

"Where is he?" Tomás asked, taking the cross from her.

The woman looked quickly about. Don Solá could not be seen. She led Tomás across the yard to a small shed.

"In here," she said in a low voice.

Tomás went into the dark shed and closed the door behind him.

"Rosario," he called softly. "Where are you? It is Tomás."

The Indian boy came out from his hiding place. "Help me to get out of here," he said. "María lived at our mission. She knows me. She hid me here. But I must get away. If Don Solá finds me, he will kill me."

"Rosario, you are hurt!" Tomás said. "There is blood all over your arm."

"It is nothing. I will be all right," answered Rosario. "Tell Father Salazar that I did not want to run away. The others made me do it. They found out that I knew of their plans. They have all gone to the hills. I was hurt and could not follow them."

"Tell him yourself," Tomás told the boy. "Come on. We must get back to the mission and take care of that arm."

But the Indian boy held back. "No, wait," he said. "I have been thinking. I think that I won't go back. It is hard to know what to do. I have learned the white man's ways—I have never known any other life. Yet, at heart, I am still Indian. When I look at the hills, part of me longs to be free—to live in the old ways of my people. I want to be as you are, Tomás—free to go as I please."

"Rosario!" Tomás cried. "Your people are not free. They are only wild. They live almost like the poor animals. Someday the white man will take even the hills away from them. Those who live in the old ways will be lost. In the hills, there is nothing but hunger and death for you. Come back to the mission, Rosario. That is where you belong."

The Indian boy said nothing. He stood, staring at his feet. Tomás took the wooden cross. He tied it about the boy's neck.

"Rosario, look at me," he begged. "Why do you

think I go from one place to the next? Because I want to? No! It is because I have no home. There is no one who cares for me at La Paz—no one waiting for me to return. But you—*you* have a place at the mission. You are needed. Father Salazar can't believe that you have left him."

At that, Rosario looked up. His eyes were bright. "Yes, you are right, Tomás," he said slowly. "I must go back."

With Rosario behind him, Tomás opened the door. He looked right into the angry face of Don Solá!

"So!" the ranchero said. "You thought to play tricks on Don Solá! Give me that Indian. I will teach him to steal from me."

"This boy took nothing, Señor. He belongs to the mission. If you hurt him, there will be trouble," Tomás warned.

Don Solá shook his fist. He knew that Tomás was right. The rancheros could use the land for their cattle. But they could not bother the mission or the mission Indians.

"Then get off my land—both of you," Don Solá cried.

The two boys were glad enough to get away. At the big oak tree, they pulled the mare to a stop. Rosario bent over the Indian Tomás had left there. The man was still alive, but very weak.

"This one belongs to the church," Rosario said. "Help me, Tomás. We must take him back to Father Salazar."

Together, the boys lifted the Indian. They tied him across the mare's back.

As they walked on, Tomás asked, "Isn't Don Solá friendly with Father Salazar?"

"Father Salazar does not like to have the rancho here," Rosario said slowly. "He says that the King of Spain has promised to give us Indians land of our own. But he is afraid that the rancheros will take all the land. Then there will be none left for us Indians."

Suddenly, Tomás thought of his black pearl. "What did you do with my clothing?" he asked.

"Why, I gave it to the women to wash. Isn't that what you wanted me to do?"

Tomás groaned. Only a miracle would help him find the pearl now.

5

When they reached the mission, Rosario went at once to find Father Salazar. Tomás waited in the patio. Beyond the walls, the men were making adobe bricks. They mixed the mud, straw, and sand with their bare feet. They sang as they worked. Their feet kept time to their Indian song.

Tomás heard the weavers at their looms. He heard the hum of women's voices. They were sitting in the sun, near the kitchen. They were grinding corn. Every now and then, they stopped to shoo away a chicken.

Tomás listened to the sound of their *metates*. He had an idea.

"The *metate* is slow," he thought. "Father Salazar needs a water wheel to grind his grain. I'd like to build a water wheel for him."

Tomás looked about him at the young fruit trees, at the pink roses growing over the patio walls. Only yesterday, this mission had seemed a wild and lonely place. It had seemed like the end of the world.

But now he thought, "It is really the beginning of a new world—a new Spain."

"Tomás," a soft voice said.

The boy turned to find Father Salazar beside him. "Rosario has told me everything. He has told me why he left. He has also told me why he came back. You did your job well. You used your head and your heart to bring him back. The soldiers would have used a whip."

"Yes," said Tomás. "The whip is no good for the Indian. It only teaches him to hate."

Father Salazar smiled and said, "You will make a good leader someday, Tomás. But before I forget—here is something that belongs to you."

Father Salazar held out his hand. In it lay the shining pearl.

"There is a figure of the Holy Mother in our church," he said. "I found the pearl lying at her feet. One of the Indian women found it earlier. She did not know that it belonged to you. She took it to the church, as a gift."

Tomás held the pearl up to the sunlight. He looked at it a long time. "I used to say to myself, 'It doesn't matter what anyone thinks of me. I have a fine pearl.' I used to think I wouldn't trade my pearl for anything on earth."

Father Salazar smiled. "The world is full of good things, my son," he said. "When you find them, you will no longer need the pearl to make you happy. But I have good news for you. Father Ávila is on his way home. You may have a horse tomorrow."

"Then I can get my Josefa," cried Tomás. "That is good news!"

"Good news for you, but not for us," said Father Salazar. "We had hoped that you would stay a little longer. You know, Rosario is praying for another miracle. He is praying that you will come and live here at the mission."

"Oh, that foolish Rosario and his miracles!" said Tomás, laughing. Then he remembered the first time he had met the Indian boy. He sighed.

"I may as well give up," he said. "What chance have I against Rosario's prayer? Tell him I will come back."

The next day Tomás set off to get Josefa. Rosario went to the gate with him.

"Here are fruits and cheese to eat on the way," the Indian boy said. "Do not be gone too long."

Tomás said, "I will hurry back. But wait! Give this to Father Salazar."

Tomás took the black pearl from his belt and gave it to Rosario.

"Now the good father will not have to worry about money for Spain. He can send this to the King. Tell him I don't need it now. He will understand."

Rosario looked at the pearl. He did not know what to make of it. *"This?* For the King? But it is only a little gray stone," he said.

Tomás rode away, laughing at Rosario's words. He turned once and looked back at the mission. It was a pretty sight in the warm sunlight. The bells were ringing. The Indians were starting toward the fields.

"Who cares for a little gray stone?" he thought, smiling to himself. "There is work to be done. There are good friends waiting. I'll hurry back."

Under Mexican Rule

FOR many years, Mexico and the Californias belonged to Spain. But the people were restless and unhappy. They did not like being ruled by a faraway king.

The King of Spain would not let the Californians trade with other countries. He would not send them the things they needed. Pirates were robbing and burning their pueblos. The soldiers had no guns to fight them off.

At last Mexico won its freedom from Spain. California became a part of the new Republic of Mexico. At once, things began to change!

The mission lands were given to the people. By 1836 there were many large ranchos in California. The pueblos were growing. Ships brought goods from all over the world to trade for California hides and tallow.

"The Magic Door" is a story of those days when California was just beginning to grow.

THE MAGIC DOOR

1

The rancho was waking up. One last star hung in the sky. But morning was coming over the hills.

The Indians were already leaving their huts. They were going up the hill to the big adobe ranch house. They walked quietly on bare feet. They soon filled the wide courtyard. They waited there, talking in low voices. When the ranchero and his family came downstairs, morning prayers would begin.

The family was already starting down the steps from the long, covered porch above. First came Don Carlos and Doña Teresa. The boys followed. There were six of them—Ramón, Antonio, Juan, José, Fermín, and Benito.

But where was Luisa? She was the youngest of the family, and the only girl. The other Indians looked at Inez, who was Luisa's servant.

"Where's the little one?" they asked. "Is she sick?"

Inez shook her head. "Not that one! If I know my Luisa, she is up to her old tricks."

As soon as prayers were over, the Indian woman hurried to Luisa's room. She took a pot of chocolate and some *tortillas* with her. At the door, she stopped and sighed. She never knew just what she would find when she walked into that room!

Luisa was standing in the middle of her bed, putting on her clothes. But they were not *her* clothes. They were Benito's. She pulled on the long black pants. She buttoned up the white shirt and put on the short coat. She tied a bright sash around her waist and jumped off the bed to hunt for shoes.

Inez set the tray down. She put her hands on her hips.

"Now just where do you think you are going, dressed that way?" she asked.

"Why—to the *matanza,* of course," said Luisa.

"Last night your father said—"

"He said he *wished* that I would spend more time learning to sew and to run the house. He didn't say I could not go to the *matanza.* Come on, Inez. I'll eat while you comb my hair. Put it up on top of my head, so that Benito's hat will hide it. I'll look like one of the boys. Father will never even know I'm there."

Inez sighed and picked up the brush. She looked into the mirror at the girl's shining eyes and rosy cheeks. "You did not come down for prayers. Did you tell your poor mother that you were sick again?"

"Well, it was *almost* the truth," Luisa said. "Every time I think of sitting and sewing, it makes my head hurt."

"Oh, Luisa, Luisa," the Indian woman said sadly. "Will you ever grow up? Now look at your cousin. She is only three years older than you. She already has a fine husband and a nice home. But *you*—Luisa, you must stop fighting what is meant to be. You are making yourself and everyone else unhappy."

"Ouch!" cried Luisa crossly. "You are pulling my hair. 'Grow up, grow up, grow up!' That is all I hear, and I'm sick of it! See who is in the courtyard now."

Inez went to the door and looked down. "Only a few women leading the carts," she said. "They are going to the river to wash today."

Luisa finished the last bite of *tortilla*. She pulled on Benito's wide hat. She was soon down the steps and on her horse.

"Be careful," Inez called after her.

But Luisa was already too far away to hear. Her horse ran swiftly. His head was low, his mane flying. Faster and faster they raced, over the rolling hills. At last Luisa pulled the horse to a stop. She could see the cattle and riders now. The *matanza* was beginning.

Luisa could hear the thunder of hoofs. Whips cracked! Men yelled! The cattle were moving about. An Indian rode into the herd at top speed. He held a knife high in the air. As he passed each animal, he brought the knife down on the back of its neck. The animal fell and did not move.

Both the men and the horses had to know their job well. The cattle were half wild. They were never fenced, but ran free all year. There were thousands of them on the rancho.

Now more Indians were moving in. These were the skinners. They would take the hides off the dead animals.

But there was trouble at the far end of the field! Many of the cattle had been driven off. They moved together at the end of the field. One old bull started to run. Others followed. A hundred wild cattle were soon pounding across the field.

"A stampede!" cried Luisa.

Don Carlos had seen it, too. "Head them off!" he yelled. "Keep them away from the skinners. Drive them to the river."

Luisa saw her brothers and the Indians riding hard. Finally they were able to turn the cattle. The animals were still running at full speed.

"The women are at the river today," Luisa thought. "They will all be killed!"

The cattle were heading straight for the washing place. Luisa knew that she must warn her father before it was too late. She dug her heels into her horse's

ribs. To reach her father, she must cross in front of the cattle. There was no time to lose. They were coming fast.

Benito's hat slid down Luisa's back. Her long hair was flying in the wind. Now she was in front of the wild herd. The pounding of the cattle's hoofs was like thunder. Closer and closer came the animals' long, cruel horns. If her horse should fall now—!

But in a moment, Luisa was safe on the other side. The animals went thundering past her. She reached her father's side.

"Drive them south!" she cried. "The women are at the river, washing."

Don Carlos did not stop for words. His pale, angry face said enough. He rode off at top speed, yelling his orders to the others. The sound of pounding hoofs died away. Luisa saw the great cloud of dust moving to the south. She knew that the women would be safe.

The girl pushed the long hair away from her face and put her hat back on her head. "They are safe," she thought. "And I am in for trouble!"

2

Luisa rode back across the field. She passed the skinners, still at work. Other Indians were moving in among the dead animals. They were cutting up the best of the beef for drying. The women would come now, with bags made of hide. They would fill their bags with fat for making candles and soap.

Birds flew overhead. A pack of hungry dogs waited on the hill. It would soon be their turn to feast. That night the bears would eat what the dogs had left.

Luisa had seen enough of the *matanza*. She turned toward home.

"You are as white as a ghost," cried Inez when she saw the girl.

Luisa pulled off Benito's dusty clothing. She put on a clean white blouse and a skirt. Inez brought water to bathe the girl's face and arms. She brushed Luisa's long, black curls once more.

"Did Don Carlos see you?" Inez asked.

"Yes, and he was angry," Luisa said. She told the Indian woman about the stampede.

Inez shook her head sadly. "Oh, Luisa! You will be eating on your knees for *weeks*."

Inez was right. When Luisa went down to dinner, there was no place set for her at the table. She looked over into the corner of the room. Yes, there was the stool. There was the tin cup, the wooden spoon, and the old, broken dish. She walked slowly to the corner and got down on her knees before the stool.

Luisa's face was to the wall. She could not see her father. But she knew that he was very angry. The others were not talking or laughing. Even gay Benito could not find a word to say.

The servants brought Luisa soup and big pieces of beef. But nothing tasted good to her. She felt that she would burn up with shame.

As soon as their father had left the room, the boys ran to Luisa's side.

"It is not fair," Benito cried. "You were very brave today. But for you, the women at the river would be dead!"

The others nodded. But Luisa had only tears for an answer. She ran to her room to cry alone. Much later, Inez brought in her supper on a tray.

Luisa took the fruit and tea to her bedroom door. She could sit there and look at the bright stars. The cool night air felt good on her hot cheeks. The boys were singing and playing their guitars. The unhappy girl listened to the sweet music for a long time.

Suddenly, Luisa heard her father's heavy step in the courtyard below. Then she heard the tap-tap of high wooden heels, and her mother's voice.

"Carlos, Carlos! Sometimes I think that you are blind."

"I see this much," said Don Carlos in an angry voice. "Luisa is growing older. She will soon be old enough to marry. Yet she knows nothing of a woman's work. Nor does she care to learn!"

Doña Teresa sighed and said, "Luisa has courage. She has a loving heart and willing hands. She will make a good wife and a good mother. When the time comes for her to marry, she will learn the other things."

"Bah!" said Don Carlos. "You should have seen her today, Teresa. She is as wild as a rabbit, and ten times more foolish. Do you think any man will want a—a lady *vaquero* for a wife? One who does not know one end of a needle from the other?"

"But she has grown up with six boys," said Luisa's mother. "Of course, she likes to do as they do. It is lonely for her, just sitting and sewing all by herself."

"Then there is only one thing to do," said Don Carlos. "We'll send her to the hacienda. She can spend a year with her cousins. They are little ladies, all of them. Perhaps they will be able to make a lady of Luisa, too."

Luisa had heard enough! She closed her door quickly. "A *year*—a whole year—with those silly cousins!" she cried. "No. I won't do it! I'll *never* leave the rancho. They *can't* send me away!"

But in her heart Luisa knew that she would have to go. The word of Don Carlos was law in his family.

Inez came in to prepare Luisa's bed for the night. She turned back the heavy silk cover and shook up the pillows. She put Luisa's nightclothes on the bed. "Come now," she said softly. "It has been a bad day for you, little one. It's time for you to go to sleep."

"They are sending me away, Inez," the girl sobbed.

"I know. I heard it. Oh, Luisa! I knew that you would go too far someday. I tried to warn you."

Inez left, and Luisa's mother came into the room to put out the candles. Luisa hid her face in the pillow. She could not talk to anyone tonight—not even her mother. She was glad when the door closed, and she was alone.

Luisa heard the key turn in the lock. It was the last sound she heard each night—the first one each morning. The lower rooms were never locked. They were always open to friend or stranger. But Mexican children went to their rooms soon after supper, and their doors were locked. Each father saw his sons safely into bed. Each mother locked her girls in for the night.

Luisa turned over and watched the shadows on the wall. "And I used to think that twelve would be such a nice age," she thought. "But I hate it! It's too young for this, and too old for that. Will I ever, *ever* be just the right age for *anything?*"

3

The next morning Luisa was still angry. Her eyes were red from crying.

Inez took one look at her and said, "Listen to me, child. Tears and anger will not help. You had better be thinking of ways to please your father. Perhaps he will change his mind if he sees that you are trying."

Luisa put a wet cloth over her eyes. What could she

do to please Don Carlos? She had only a little time. He had said that she was as wild and as foolish as a rabbit. Surely he would not change his mind overnight.

But Luisa had no more time for thinking then. The courtyard was suddenly filled with noise. A stranger came riding in, followed by a pack of barking dogs. Luisa and Inez ran to the porch and leaned over the railing.

"The Yankee ship has come!" said Luisa. "That man is the agent. I have seen him here before."

The trading ship came every few months. It stopped at ports along the California coast to pick up hides and tallow. Don Carlos traded his cattle hides to the Yankees and got wonderful things in return. Now that the ship was in, he would be in a happy mood!

"The hides will keep Don Carlos busy for the next week," said Inez.

Luisa smiled for the first time. "Too busy to think of me, I hope," she said. "Maybe Mother will take us down to the ship." Her eyes were shining now.

The ships that came from Boston were full of wonderful things—silks and cotton cloth, shawls and shoes and stockings. They brought in farm tools and furniture, and a hundred other things. When a ship came into port, everyone came from miles around. Those who had no hides to trade came anyway—just to look.

There was hardly a store in all California. The only place to buy such things was from a trading ship.

Don Carlos was already giving orders to his sons. "Bring the men from the fields! Open the storehouse! Be sure that all the tallow and hides are taken out. And you, Ramón, see that the carts are ready. We'll start loading them right away."

One after the other, the carts rolled away. They were piled high with hides. Their heavy wooden wheels made a great noise. Indians walked beside

them, poking the slow oxen with sharp sticks. As always, a dozen barking dogs ran behind.

Luisa looked on from the cool porch. Once her mother came into the courtyard and called up to her, "Ramón will take us to the ship tomorrow. Tell Inez to be ready to leave early."

Ramón was Luisa's oldest brother. Next to their father and mother, he was the most important member of the family. He was given many of the jobs that Don Carlos did not have time to do.

Early the next day, Ramón rode beside his mother to the river. Luisa and Inez went along. Doña Teresa had brought along her own servant. When they came back, there would be many things to carry. The riders waited on their horses while the Yankee sailors loaded a small boat.

There was still a great pile of hides on the riverbank—and more to come! The sailors slid up and down the muddy riverbank. Each of them carried two of the cattle hides on top of his head.

Doña Teresa looked down at her dress. She was wearing her best black silk and her lace shawl.

"We are going to be a fine sight!" she said, laughing. "All dressed up, and riding on a pile of old hides."

But the sailors saved a place for Luisa and her mother at the end of the boat. Before long, the party was being rowed down the river and out into the blue bay. When they reached the trading ship, they found that it was packed with people. There was much laughing and talking aboard. A big room below deck had been turned into a store. A Yankee sailor was the clerk.

"You will need new dresses for your visit, Luisa," her mother said. "Come. Help me pick out some pretty cloth."

Luisa tried to be excited about the new dresses. But it was no use. She could not bear to think about a year at the hacienda. She sat down on a barrel beside Inez. Doña Teresa looked over the piles of silk and cotton cloth. Luisa touched one of the pieces of silk. It was soft and fine and white.

"Oh, not that, Luisa," said her mother. "Choose something with a little color."

But Luisa was not thinking of a dress for herself. She was thinking of something Inez had said—about pleasing her father.

"Please, Mother, get the white silk," the girl said. "I want enough to make Father a shirt."

Doña Teresa's eyes grew wide. *"A shirt!* But—." Doña Teresa found a dozen things wrong with her daughter's plan. The main one, of course, was that Luisa could not sew. But, in the end, she gave in. The white silk was put with the other things she was buying.

As the family turned to leave, they heard a well-known voice. "Teresa! Luisa! Ramón! It is good to see you."

And there was Luisa's uncle from the hacienda— Don Pío! The grownups talked and talked. Luisa stood first on one foot, then on the other. She wanted to hurry home and start work on her father's shirt. But Don Pío would not hear of their going home.

"No, no," he said. "You would not get home before dark. The hacienda is much closer. Besides, we are having a big party tonight. Everyone is coming."

"But who will tell Father?" asked Luisa. "He will worry."

"There is still work for me at the rancho," Ramón said. "I must go back anyway. I will tell him."

Luisa gave her brother a black look. She did not want to spend time at the hacienda now. After all, she had a year of it to look forward to.

But Ramón whispered, "Don't be foolish. Go. Stay as long as you can. Perhaps Father will cool off before you get home."

Luisa sighed. Perhaps Ramón was right. Two weeks now would be easier than a whole year later on. And she would find time to work on the shirt while she was there.

Poor Luisa! She did not know it then, but it would be a long, long time before that silk shirt was finished.

4

Another small boat took the shoppers to the shore. Don Pío lifted Doña Teresa onto his horse, and jumped on behind her. Luisa and the servants rode in his cart. They bumped along through the tiny pueblo. The streets were filled with people. There was always excitement when a trading ship was in the bay.

The travelers left the pueblo behind and rode across the brown hills. Now and then, they rode through groves of oak and pine. Rabbits jumped, and ran to miss the noisy cartwheels. Birds flew to safety in the treetops.

At last the party reached Don Pío's hacienda. Luisa sat up and rubbed her eyes. "Mmmm," she said. "Something smells good. It makes me hungry."

"There is a bull cooking in the pit," said her uncle, smiling. He helped her from the cart. "If you like to eat and dance, you will enjoy yourself tonight!"

Before the sun went down, guests began coming. Luisa saw the dust rising far down the road. The house and gardens were soon full of people.

"Luisa! You have not spoken to your cousins yet," her mother said. "Go and do so!"

Luisa sighed. Don Pío's four girls were only a little

older than she. The oldest one was already married. But the other three gave her trouble enough! Hardly a day went by that she did not hear of "Don Pío's girls." They seemed to be all that she could not be.

Doña Teresa gave Luisa a little push. The girl walked over to her three cousins. In a very small voice, she said, *"Buenos días."*

"See how tall Luisa has grown," said one of the girls. "She is taller than I now."

"Yes," said another, smiling. "If we are not careful, she will have all the dances tonight."

Luisa felt angry and mixed up. Her cousins were so silly! She did not know how to answer them. She was glad that it would soon be time to eat.

Long tables were set under the trees. They were loaded with food of all kinds—beef, chickens, vegetables, and fruits. After everyone had eaten, they rested awhile. Then the dancing began.

The dirt in the courtyard was hard and smooth. It made a good place to dance. Don Pío led each of the ladies out to the center. He danced a few steps with each of them. At first only the older people danced. The others sat on their horses, or on low benches, and looked on.

But soon, everyone was dancing. Even the small children were hopping about to the music. One little girl was dancing with her grandfather.

"Last year I could dance with the little ones and have fun," Luisa thought. "But I would look foolish doing so now."

The moon rose higher and higher. The torches burned low. Watching the dancers made Luisa dizzy. Their wide skirts were spinning as quickly and gaily as butterfly wings. Luisa saw her cousins trying to teach a blue-eyed Yankee a new step. They were all laughing and having fun—all but Luisa, who sat alone in the shadows.

At last Luisa could stand it no longer. She ran to her room and threw herself onto the bed, crying.

In a moment, Doña Teresa came into the room. "What is it?" she asked. "What is it, Luisa?"

"I hate parties," sobbed Luisa. "That Don Pío! He said I would have fun. It was nothing but a big lie!"

Luisa felt her mother's hand on her hair. Finally she sat up and wiped away her tears. Doña Teresa put out the candles. She put her arm around the girl and drew her to the window.

"Come and look, Luisa," she said softly. "Do you see? The world does not look the same at night as it does during the day. But the sun does not lie. Nor does the moon. All the things that seem so hard and hateful to you now will seem different in a little while."

Luisa looked out of the window. The moon had turned the world to silver. The trees looked as though they had been painted on the hills. Nothing moved at all, nothing but the tiny stars. There was something that Luisa wanted to ask her mother. It was hard to find the words. Finally they came out.

"How do you grow up?" she asked. "Is it something magic that happens all of a sudden?"

"Maybe it is a little like magic—like finding a magic door," her mother answered. "Something makes you want to find out what is on the other side. Yet you know that you can never come back, once you have gone through that door."

Luisa almost stopped breathing. Yes, that was just the way she felt.

"And then what?" she asked.

Doña Teresa smiled and said, "Someday you will wake up and find that the door has closed behind you. Just like that! There are other magic doors, even beyond that one. But the growing-up door is harder to go through than all the rest."

Luisa sighed. She was not sure that she knew any more than she had before.

"Now you want me to tell you *how* to get through the door," her mother said, laughing. "But I can't tell you that. It is different for everyone. Come now. It is time that we were both in bed."

The days that followed were quiet. Luisa, her mother, and her cousins went to church at the old mission near the pueblo. Luisa began to work on her father's shirt. She rode over Don Pío's land. The hacienda was not at all like the rancho. Here fruits and grains grew everywhere. It was beautiful. But Luisa could not help wanting to be back home.

Luisa rode in from the fields one day. She found Don Pío packing horses for their trip home.

"I didn't know that we were leaving today," said Luisa.

"Inez has told us of trouble at home," said Doña Teresa. Her face was pale and worried.

"But how could Inez know that? Did someone send word from the rancho?" Luisa asked.

Her mother shook her head. "No, Inez only says that she knows there is trouble. Perhaps it is foolish to believe such things. But I cannot rest now until we are at home."

Luisa remembered something that her father had told her long ago. In mission days, only a few ships ever came to California. The soldiers and the priests never knew when a ship would come into port. But the Indians knew! They knew that the ship was coming many days before the sails were ever seen.

Suddenly Luisa was afraid.

5

It was a long, long ride to the rancho. Luisa's party had to go around the bay. Then they must cross the river before they would be on her father's land. Don Pío rode with them to the river. He had sent an Indian ahead to tell Ramón to meet them there.

But when they reached the river, Ramón was not there.

"You need not come farther, Pío," Doña Teresa said. "I know that you must go back to your harvest. We'll be quite safe from here on."

The riders said good-by to Don Pío. It was sundown before they saw the ranch house. Inez pointed to the black smoke rising from the Indian huts.

"Look!" she said in a low voice. "They are burning the homes of the dead. The white man's sickness has come again."

Smallpox! In times before, the sickness had swept through California. The white men did not catch it easily. But their Indian brothers died by the hundreds. Whole villages were wiped out. Inez was the only one of her family who had lived.

It was not long until they reached the ranch house. The big courtyard was empty. Luisa looked around sadly. There had always been someone waiting there to care for the horses. There had always been women grinding corn. Now the grinding stones were lying in the dirt. And there was no one—no one anywhere, it seemed.

Doña Teresa jumped from her horse and ran into the kitchen. Luisa and Inez followed her.

"Look!" cried Luisa. "The fires are out. No one has been in the kitchen for days."

Her mother leaned against the wall. There were tears in her eyes. "What can we do?" she cried. "There is no one to cook for the family. No one to grind the corn—no one to do anything."

Luisa put her hands on her hips. "Well then, you

and I will have to do it," she said quietly. "It must be done. Come on, let's start the fires."

"You are right," said her mother. "There is no time for crying. We must make soup right away— enough to feed the sick tonight. Heaven only knows what they have been eating." Then she began to give orders.

"Go down to the huts, Inez. Find out how many people we have lost, and how many are left. Tell Don Carlos that we are at home. And tell Benito I want clean straw brought to the storehouse."

"Yes, the storehouse would be a good place to care for the sick," said Luisa.

When the pots of soup were cooking, Inez came back. "It is bad—very bad," she said. "Only a few are left, and they are very sick. Don Carlos and the boys have been digging graves all day. Benito is bringing the straw, as you asked."

"Oh, Inez!" Luisa took the Indian woman's hand. "But come. Perhaps we can save those who are still alive. Help me to take some sheets to the storehouse. And bring a broom. We'll soon have beds ready. The boys can move the sick tonight."

The next few weeks were terrible. There was little sleep for anyone. Those who were well hardly had time to eat. The family did the work that fifty Indians had done before. Inez did what she could to help. But she had only been trained to care for Luisa.

And so it was Luisa who sat in the courtyard, grinding the corn. It was Luisa who helped to care for the sick. One morning she looked up to find her father beside her. He pushed back his hat and sat down. He took the stone from her and looked at her small hands. They were rough and dirty. Every fingernail was broken.

Don Carlos shook his head sadly. "When I was a boy, we lived in Sonora," he said. "We were very poor. My mother and father did the hardest kind of work to keep us alive. Ah, it hurt me to see them. I said then that I would grow up to be a rich man. I never again wanted to see those I loved working so hard. And now—"

Poor Don Carlos! Luisa was sorry for him. Everything had gone wrong. She looked down at her dirty hands and thought of Don Pío's pretty girls. "Don't worry," she said. "I do not mind the work. The bad times will soon be over. You will see. And when there is time, I'll finish making a gift I have for you. You're going to be surprised when you see it."

Her father smiled. Doña Teresa had told him of the silk shirt. Now he thought of something else she had once said. "Courage—a loving heart—willing hands," he said slowly. "Those are the best gifts of all. And you give them every day, Luisa. I have always loved my children. But I never knew how much—until now."

It was late that night when the day's work was done. Luisa went slowly up the steps to her room. She lighted the candles and turned back the covers on her bed. She washed with water from the jug. Then she sat down before the mirror to brush her hair. In a few moments, she heard a soft step behind her.

"Inez, you did not need to come tonight," she said. "You are tired. I am able to brush my own hair, you know."

Inez took the brush from Luisa's hand and said, "No. Let me. I have not done this in a long time, and I want to do it again."

Inez lifted Luisa's long, black hair and drew the

brush through it. The two looked at each other in the mirror.

"What is it?" Luisa asked. "You are looking so strange."

"I was looking for a little girl I once knew," Inez said slowly. "But she is gone."

Luisa looked into the mirror. But she saw nothing. It was as though she were blind for a moment. The door—the magic door—had closed behind her. And the place beyond was not strange at all. She was closer to her family than she had ever been before—and happier.

Inez gathered the shining hair into a knot and fastened it up with a comb. "See how you will look with your hair done up," she said, smiling. "Just think, in

a few years you will have a home of your own. I'll come with you and take care of your children. You will be my Doña Luisa."

Yes, there were many doors ahead—many magic doors. But Luisa knew that she would never again be afraid. Beyond each door she would find a new kind of happiness.

When Wagon Wheels Rolled

STRANGERS began to drift into California—trappers and traders, sailors and settlers. America was moving westward.

During these years, there was trouble between Mexico and the United States. When the two countries made peace, they agreed that California should be a part of the United States.

Then gold was discovered! From every corner of the earth, gold-hungry men hurried to California. They came on foot, on muleback, by ship, and by wagon train. Towns and cities grew up in the valleys. Mining camps sprang up in the hills. Almost overnight California became a busy, crowded place.

"Go West for Gold!" is about an American family who joined the gold rush in 1850. It is the story of their search and their adventures—and of the gold they finally found.

GO WEST FOR GOLD!

1

"Jed, listen!" Sally whispered to her brother. "Do you hear it?"

Jed sat up. He was careful not to waken Baby Sue. She slept between them in the wagon. At first, Jed heard only the canvas cover of the wagon snapping in the wind.

"Now I do," he whispered. "Sounds like a horse. It's coming closer!"

"Oh, I hope it's Pa," Sally said.

Pa and Big Sam had been sent ahead to find the pass for the wagon train. That had been two days ago. Big Sam had come back, but Pa had not.

The horse stopped beside the Winters' wagon. Its rider was Captain Small, leader of the wagon train.

"We have to move on tomorrow, Ma'am," he said.

"Without Mr. Winters? Can't we wait one more day?" Ma cried.

"I'm sorry, Ma'am. We sent men to look for him," Captain Small said. "We know that he's not in those hills. I can't hold those people here an hour longer."

"Gold! They just want to get their hands on that gold. A man's life is worth nothing!" Ma was angry.

"I don't look at it that way, Ma'am," Captain Small said. "There are other lives to think of, too. We have to get over the top before the snow hits. That means we must get moving—and keep moving."

At last Ma said, "All right. I reckon that's the only thing to do."

The horseman rode off. Jed took Sally's hand.

"Don't cry, Sal," he whispered. "Maybe Pa isn't dead. Maybe he's waiting for us—somewhere over the mountain."

Ma lay down with the children under the buffalo robe.

She said, "Your Pa is not a man to give up easily. You keep believing that. And keep praying."

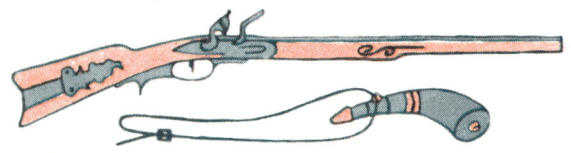

"Stretch out—stretch out!"

Back in Independence, Missouri, every heart had welcomed that cry. Now, tired men and tired animals lifted their heads to the call. Even the wagons seemed to groan more loudly as they moved into line.

Jed wiped the sweat from his eyes. "There they are," he said. "The mountains, the Sierra Nevada, Sally. And look at that snow!"

"Oh, Jed, sometimes I wonder whether we will ever get to California," said Sally. "What if we get snowed in, up at the pass?"

"Hush, now. Don't let Ma hear you talk like that. She has enough on her mind. Captain Small says, with any luck at all, we ought to make it."

"We haven't been very lucky so far," Sally said.

She was thinking of the desert they had just crossed. Broken wagons and dead animals marked the path across the sand. The trip was a nightmare of heat and thirst. Two of their friends had died there. Two sticks in the sand marked the children's lonely graves. Both Sally and Jed were remembering their lost friends.

"Well, at least we are still alive. And as long as we follow the Carson River, we'll have plenty of wood and water," said Jed.

"I'd feel better if we had more food in that wagon," Sally said. "I looked in the cornmeal barrel this morning. I'll bet there isn't a handful left."

Hundreds of wagons had already crossed the plains. Coming late in 1850, Captain Small's train found little grass left. Firewood, too, was hard to find. When they could not find wood, they burned buffalo chips.

Even the hunting was poor. The elk, deer, and buffalo had learned to fear the wagon trains.

"Oh, shucks! What is the matter with these mules now?" Jed snapped his whip over the tired animals. "Gee, Babe! Gee, Brandy!" he yelled to the lead mules.

But the mules would not move a step. They tossed their heads and put their long ears forward. Jed and Sally had learned to watch those long ears. They warned when wild animals or Indians were near.

"Look there," Jed said suddenly.

A puff of dust moved across the top of a low hill. Sally could see a horse and rider, going at top speed. The horseman rode off into the cottonwood trees, and was lost from sight—but not before Jed and Sally had had a good look at the horse.

"That was Pa's horse!" Sally cried out. "I saw it as plain as anything."

2

"That was Pa's horse all right," Jed said. "But an Indian was riding it!" The boy's face was dead white. Never before had he felt so lonely and sad.

"Better get the team going, son," Ma called. She was feeding Baby Sue inside the wagon.

Jed said in a low voice, "Don't you let on to Ma about this. She has to keep believing that Pa is still alive."

The children walked on sadly. Their terrible secret kept them silent. The trail was rougher now. They had left the sandy plains, the sage and cottonwood trees. Tall pines and big rocks rose on every side. It was not long before Captain Small ordered the party to stop and empty their wagons. They loaded their belongings on the extra mules.

Sally had trouble putting her pack on a mule's back. Then the mule rubbed against a tree. The pack slid under its ribs.

"It's plain to see why men cuss mules," she said.

"Well, just you remember, ladies don't," Ma told her.

Ma, Sally, and Sue went ahead with the pack mules. Jed stayed with the men to help get the wagons over the rocks. With their backs to the wheels,

the men and boys tugged and lifted. Finally the last wagon was helped over the big rocks.

Ma cooked salt pork and the last of the cornmeal for supper.

"My, but that pine wood makes a good fire," she said, hugging her sleepy baby. "A body can forget a heap of trouble beside a nice warm fire."

The plunk-plunk of a banjo started. Someone began playing "Sweet Betsy from Pike." Soon everyone was singing.

Captain Small rode up. "I'll need extra men to

stand watch tonight. How about you, Jed?" he asked.

Jed picked up Pa's long rifle. "Be glad to, sir."

Captain Small put a hand on the boy's arm. "The Indians may try to make off with our mules, son. But they won't hurt us if we don't hurt them. So don't shoot to kill."

Jed thought of the Indian on Pa's horse. He longed to even up the score. But orders were orders.

Captain Small went on talking. "I have some bad news, Ma'am. The trail ahead is pretty bad. I reckon we'll have to leave our wagons here."

"But other wagons have made it," Ma cried. "Why can't ours?"

"Wagons will slow us down. Every hour counts, until we get through that pass, Ma'am."

Ma closed her eyes to keep back the tears. Pa had made that wagon with his own hands! It still held his plow and the butter churn. The big trunk filled with their extra clothing was in the wagon. So were all the seeds to start a new garden, and her hand-made quilts. A bolt of muslin and one of calico, the Dutch oven, the coffee grinder, her flatirons, and her very best hair-filled mattress—all were in the wagon.

Of course, they could not carry all that on the mules. It could not be done!

Ma put her hands on her hips. She looked Captain Small straight in the eye.

"Sir, I've lost all that I mean to lose," she said. "This wagon is the only home we've got. My baby would die of the cold without it. No, sir, I'm keeping this wagon! I aim to take Mr. Winters his plow and our family things—all of them!"

Jed and Sally looked at each other. Poor Ma! She still thought that Pa was alive.

Jed spoke up. "You all go along if you want to, sir. We'll get to California. And we'll get there all of a piece."

Four other families decided to keep their wagons. The rest loaded their most needed belongings on mules. They started up the trail and were soon out of sight.

The trail suddenly ended at the foot of a small cliff. "Now what?" Jed asked himself. But Big Sam knew what to do. The men loaded the pack mules again. They rigged up a pulley. They tied ropes to the wagons. Both the mules and the men sweated and tugged. Finally the empty wagons were lifted up the cliff, one by one.

"We did it! And we didn't lose a single wagon," said Jed, turning to Big Sam and grinning.

But Big Sam was lying in the dust. His face was white with pain. The men hurried to him.

"Must have hurt my back, boys. Can't seem to get on my feet," he groaned.

Big Sam rode in his wagon from that time on. The little party missed his strong arms. Ma found some painkiller and angleworm oil in the trunk. She took them to Big Sam's wife.

The woman took them without a word of thanks. "This is all your doing, Cora Winters," she said. "If it hadn't been for you, we'd be safe with Captain Small. Now we may never get out of these mountains alive."

Every morning, frost lay on the ground. Ice covered the water buckets. The little party pushed on over the rocky hill, into a narrow valley, then up and up again. They were eating the last of their dried beef. Then it began to rain. There were no fires that night. Each family ate in its own wagon and tried to keep warm.

Sally pulled the buffalo robe close about her. "This is an awfully spooky mountain," she said. "I keep hearing a funny sound—like little bells."

Then suddenly, everyone heard a loud yell.

Sally's bells were not "spook" bells. In the Sierra Nevada, most of the pack mules wore bells. The mountain trails were narrow. Often, there was not room for two pack trains to pass. The bells warned others to wait where the path was wide.

Some men and mules came around the bend. They were John Sutter's men and animals. The men had come from Sutter's Fort to help the last of the wagons over the top.

"We're saved!" Jed yelled from the wagon.

Everyone laughed and cried at the same time. Big Sam's wife hugged Ma. Tears and rain were running down her face.

"Oh, Cora!" she cried. "To think that I was so afraid. And all the time, the Lord was watching over us."

The strangers passed out flour, dried beef, beans, and coffee. One of them picked up Baby Sue and tossed her into the air.

"This one is *muy bonita*—oh, so pretty! But where are your pick and shovel, little one? You'll need them to dig for gold." The man's hair and eyes were black. His smile showed that he had strong, white teeth.

Ma said, "Back in Independence, I thought that I wanted gold. Now, all I want is a home."

"Sí, Señora," said the man. "You are wise. I am a Spaniard—a real Californio. This country is not kind to those with the gold fever. They only take from the land. They give nothing back. But I will tell you a secret about my California. Give her your heart—give her your strong arms—give her your dreams. And California will give back riches such as you have never known—to you and to your children. That I promise you, Señora."

3

"Hangtown! Mercy, what an awful name!" Sally shook the water from her homespun skirt. The rain was coming down hard. The other wagons had stopped off at the gold diggings along the American River. But Ma had had her heart set on going to Sutter's Fort.

Jed tied the mules to a tree. "Well, we can't go any farther in this rain. I see a hotel across the street," he said.

Ma, Sally, and Jed crossed the muddy street. Old

boots and empty bottles lay all around. They could hear men's voices, yelling and singing. The hotel was only a wooden frame with a canvas over the top. Ma wanted to sit down and cry.

Jed and Sally looked through the doorway. They saw bunks, a table, and some stools in the room. The place was filled with miners. Many were Spaniards, like their friend on the mountain. Most of them wore dirty red shirts and old black boots. Each man had an old felt hat pulled over his eyes. Some were playing cards. Others were dancing together. All of them had beards, and wore bowie knives and pistols in their belts. It was a wild-looking crowd.

Ma's heart sank. Mercy! She and the children could never stay in such a place!

Then the miners saw the little family. Suddenly,

the room was as quiet as a church. Finally one of the men took off his hat.

"I reckon we kind of forgot our manners, Ma'am," he said. "We don't see many ladies in these parts. You just sit here by the stove. We'll fix you a nice, hot cup of coffee."

Ma said, "Thank you, sir. But we can't stop. We're headed for Sutter's Fort."

"Why, lady, the Fort is sixty miles away," the miner said. "The trail is washed clear off the map. A mule can hardly cross the river. And if the bears didn't get you, the Indians sure enough would. You had best stay here in Hangtown until spring comes."

"*Here?* Until spring comes?" Ma cried.

Jed said, "He's right, Ma. The wagon needs fixing. The mules are worn out. We can't go on."

"Don't you worry, Ma'am. Most of the miners have gone to Sacramento for the winter. There's an empty cabin by the store. You just drink your coffee. The boys will get a fire going. You folks can move right in," he said.

When Ma and the children reached the cabin, they found a warm fire there. The miners unloaded their wagon. The men helped Ma make up beds on the dirt floor. Her trunk, churn, and wooden washtub soon stood along the wall. Boards nailed to the wall held the last of her family's food.

The man with the red beard said, "You can hang your bonnets on those pegs, Ma'am. Here's a shovel to cook on. And I figured you would want this buffalo robe hung over the door. I'll be over tomorrow, and fix you some bunks."

With tears in her eyes, Ma thanked the miners.

When they left, Sally said, "Well, you can't tell by the looks of a door what is on the other side. I never saw such wild-looking men. And I never knew kinder ones."

The family had not been in their new home long before they knew they had company—fleas! Hundreds of them! Jed woke up once during the night. A big rat was looking him in the eye. Jed pulled the covers over his head and went back to sleep. Fleas and rats were better than bears and unfriendly Indians!

The next day, Ma and Sally went to the store. Such prices! Flour sold for a dollar and a half a pound. Onions were a dollar a pound. A pound of brown sugar cost three dollars.

"Mercy! We can't pay that kind of money," Ma whispered. "I don't know how we'll ever buy food."

They went home empty-handed. Sally sat on the churn and put her chin in her hands. She thought and thought. Then she jumped up.

"Butter!" she cried. "Nice, fresh butter! I'll bet

these miners haven't seen butter in a 'coon's age. And here we are with a churn."

"A churn, but no cow. First we need money to buy a cow," Ma said.

"I could pan for gold," Jed said.

"Not in this rain, son," said Ma. "Get an empty barrel from the wagon. We'll gather all the wood ashes we can find. I'll need them for lye water. I'm going into business washing clothes. From the looks of those red shirts, Hangtown needs a woman like me."

A week later, Ma was in business. She had all the washing she could do. She was soon making a hundred dollars a week. When it rained, she had to dry the clothes inside the cabin. Jed kept the fire going, and the flatirons hot.

Rosy, the red-haired miner, rode to a nearby rancho and came back with a cow. Sally could not make butter fast enough to fill all the orders. The miners paid four dollars for every pound she could make.

The days hurried by. But Ma was not happy. One day Jed and Sally found her crying.

"I worry so about your Pa," she cried. "If he got over those mountains, I know that he headed for Sutter's Fort. We'll never find him, and he can't find us—way up here in Hangtown."

But Ma wiped away her tears very quickly. Rosy was at the door.

He asked Ma, "Do you know anything about doctoring, Ma'am? My pardner is awful sick. The doctor won't come by here for a month or more."

Ma went to the trunk for painkiller, hot pepper, blue pills, and her other medicines. She hurried away with Rosy, saying, "I'm no doctor. But I have cured a lot of sick folks. I reckon I can help your pardner."

This was the first of many such trips for Ma. Jed and Sally stayed in the cabin with Baby Sue. They kept the churn and the flatirons going. They never dreamed what a surprise was in store for them.

4

There was sickness in every camp. Ma spent many a night caring for miners sick with scurvy and fever. She would not take a penny for this. Word of her kindness was carried far over the hills. Whenever a miner was sick, his friends came to Hangtown for Ma Winters.

Ma told Jed and Sally, "It's no wonder the poor things are always sick. They wade around in cold water and sleep in the mud. They live on beans, coffee, and hardtack. What they need are fruits and greens."

Pumpkins and melons grew in the Sacramento Valley. But these foods hardly ever came into the diggings. Ma told the men how to make a tea of sassafras and hemlock leaves. This would keep them from getting scurvy.

One day, after weeks of rain, the sun came out. The air was clear and cold. Jed took one of Ma's flat pans. He started for the river.

"Hold on, son. You'd better let me show you the ropes," Rosy called. He slid down the muddy bank behind Jed.

"Where can I dig? Just any old place?" Jed asked.

Rosy laughed. "Sure—if you don't mind getting shot at. See those picks sticking up in the dirt? When you see one of those, it means that a miner has staked out a claim there. Nobody else can dig on his claim."

"Which claim is yours, Rosy?" Jed asked.

"Right over there. A man can own only one claim at a time. We figure a piece of land twenty feet long and twenty feet wide is as much as a man can work."

Jed looked at the deep holes the miners had dug. Piles of dirt and rocks were everywhere.

"Shucks! I thought you just reached in the river and took out a handful of gold," he said. "Looks like it isn't that easy."

Rosy put back his head and laughed. "The easy gold is all gone now," he said. "You have to dig down for pay dirt. Takes all day to wash ten or twelve pans of dirt. You might end up with twenty dollars' worth of gold. Or you might be lucky to find two dollars' worth in the pan. Most of us use those big Long Toms. Panning is too slow."

Jed sat down on a log. "Looks to me like Ma and Sally do better on their shirts and butter," he said.

"And so they do!" answered Rosy. "Well, anyway, you try a pan—just so you can say you did it."

When Jed got back to the cabin, he told Ma, "Some of the miners are going to Sacramento for Christmas. If the sky stays clear, the trail will be dry. We could take the wagon in."

"I think we ought to try," Ma said. "We can't stay in Hangtown forever. You children will have to go to school. We'll hit Sutter's Fort on the way. We can ask around for Pa."

At last the big day came. They were ready to go.

"Well, good-by, Hangtown," Sally said. Oh, but it would be good to see a real city again! To live near other boys and girls! The miners had been good to them. But Hangtown was a lonely place.

Jed snapped the whip and yelled, "Gee, Brandy! Gee, Babe!"

Just then a stranger rode up. He said, "I reckon you must be Ma Winters. One of our men has a bad fever. Please, Ma'am, can you come?"

Jed and Sally looked at each other. Their dream of going to Sacramento faded.

"Well, the children had their hearts set on going to Sacramento," Ma said sadly. "But—"

Sally said slowly, "You better go with him, Ma. Don't worry about us." Jed nodded that he agreed.

The two children sadly watched Ma ride off. Her blue bonnet was soon out of sight.

"We won't get to Sacramento for months now," said Jed. "By the time Ma gets back, it will be raining again. I reckon we might as well unload."

The children waited and waited. Ma did not come back. Christmas came—but no Ma Winters. The rains began again. Baby Sue cried for her mother. Jed and Sally began to feel afraid. Ma had never been gone so long before.

Then, one night, Ma stood in the doorway. She looked tired, but her eyes were bright.

"You are going to be glad we didn't go to Sacramento," she said. "I have a surprise for you!" Ma lifted the buffalo robe that hung over the door.

There stood Pa!

They all laughed and cried and hugged one another. Sally and Jed could not wait to hear Pa's story.

"Well, you remember that Big Sam and I were looking for the pass," Pa began. "He went off one way. I went the other. I got lost in the hills and—"

Jed broke in, "But what about your horse? We saw an Indian riding it. We thought you were dead."

Pa said, "Hold on a minute, son. I'm coming to that. Yes, the Indians did steal my horse. I was lucky to get away alive. I started over the mountain on foot. I thought I'd meet you at Sutter's Fort."

"And you *would* have, but for the rains," Sally said.

Pa went on. "Well, I did find out that Sutter's men had helped you over the pass. I knew you were safe, but I didn't know where. I started back along the river, but I took the wrong fork, I guess. I was running low on money when I got to the diggings. Decided to try my luck at the gold. Besides, I heard of some fine wheatland in the valley. I set my heart on buying a piece. Knew your Ma would need a place to plant that garden seed of hers."

Jed and Sally laughed. Sally said, "And Ma wouldn't move a step without your plow. That's why Captain Small went on without us."

Ma said, "All this time, your Pa has been only twenty miles away. But he was nearly dead when I

got to him. That's why I was gone so long. I didn't dare move him till he was well."

Pa said, "I've had my fill of the diggings. I want a piece of land to work."

The family talked for hours around the warm fire. They talked of the home they would build. They talked of the crops they would plant in the spring.

Many years later, the brother and sister rode over Pa's land together. They stopped their horses on a low hill. Below them lay the green and golden Central Valley of California. Herds of fat cattle grazed on the land. Jed and Sally could see roads and schools and churches. A train raced across the valley to the big city beyond.

"Remember Hangtown?" Sally asked. Most of the mining towns were dust and ashes by then. The few that stood were almost empty.

Jed smiled and said, "Yes, we came to find gold in the mountains. But the *real* gold is in our fields."

Sally nodded, looking out across the rich valley.

"And do you remember the Spaniard that night on the mountain?" Jed asked. "He told us the secret about California."

Sally said softly, "His promise came true. 'Give her your heart—give her your strong arms—give her your dreams. And California will give back riches such as you have never known.'"

Pioneers from the Far East

CALIFORNIA had many pioneers. Not all of them wore buckskin and calico. Some came from faraway China and the Pacific Islands.

By the 1860's, thousands of Chinese had come to California. They did not bring their families. They hoped to make their fortunes and return to China.

They brought with them a way of life that was already thousands of years old. Their dress, their way of worship, their food, and their customs—all were strange, indeed, to western eyes.

The Chinese helped to build roads and dikes. They dug ditches. They planted and harvested crops. They worked in factories and homes. They helped to build the great Central Pacific Railroad, which joined our country from East to West.

In "China Boy," you will meet Yat Sang, a young pioneer from the Far East.

CHINA BOY

1

"Look, there's land ahead!"

The cry was passed from one Chinese to the other. Men jumped to their feet and ran to the ship's rail. There were hundreds of them, pushing about the deck. Each wanted a first look at the strange, new land ahead.

"The golden hills! We are here at last!" cried one of the men.

Only Yat Sang hung back, listening to the high, excited voices of the others. He pushed his cold hands up into the sleeves of his thin cotton jacket.

"Golden hills, indeed!" the boy said to himself. "They look black to me."

It was all right for the others to be happy. They had paid their fare. They had jobs waiting for them in America. They would make good money. In a few years, they could return to China as rich men. But it was different for Yat Sang. The closer he came to the golden hills, the closer he came to prison.

The Chinese boy felt a hand on his arm. Again he heard the hated voice whispering, "You haven't much time now. I must have the money before the ship docks."

Yat Sang moved away from the agent. "It's no use," he said. "I don't have the money. I can't get it."

Ah Gow smiled slyly. His eyes were hard and cruel. He had made the trip from China to California many times. It was his job to bring men from the towns and farms of China to jobs in the new country. He was paid for his work. But Ah Gow knew many ways to fill his pockets with extra money. On every trip, there was someone—someone young and poor and afraid, like this Yat Sang.

Ah Gow followed the boy. "Wait," he said. "Don't be in such a hurry to run away. I'm only trying to help you."

Yat Sang kept on moving. But he could hear the voice of Ah Gow close behind him.

"Listen," the voice said. "I haven't told the captain that you came aboard without paying your fare—not yet. Your fare would cost fifty-four dollars. Give me twice that much. Then I'll keep your secret."

"What help is that?" cried Yat Sang, turning angrily. "If I couldn't pay my fare, where would I get twice as much?"

"There is one on this ship who carries much money," said Ah Gow in a low voice. "It would be easy for you to borrow a little from him."

"Borrow, indeed!" cried Yat Sang. "You mean steal. No, I won't do it!"

"Ho, ho!" said the agent, laughing. "It's a little late to think of honor. You hid on this ship, so that you could ride free. I call that stealing. So does the captain. When you're sitting in prison, you'll wish you had listened to me."

Ah Gow walked away. Yat Sang looked after him. Fear and anger were in the boy's eyes. "No! I am not a thief," he said to himself. "I didn't mean to steal. I'll pay the fare after I find work."

But who would believe him? He would be alone in a strange land, without friends or money. How could he find work if he were in prison?

The others were getting ready to land. Some of them put on clean blue jackets and black cotton pants. They rolled up their belongings in their blankets. Yat Sang had nothing but the poor rags on his back. He stood alone, looking down at the cold, gray water.

Far across the water, the lonely boy saw something moving. Could those be bamboo sails? Could they be on a Chinese boat?

"It is a junk!" cried Yat Sang. He leaned far over

the rail. The tiny junk was coming closer. He could see the fishermen moving about on the boat. One of them wore a red rag tied about his head. In China, that was the mark of the captain.

Yat Sang was thinking fast. If only he could reach the junk. He knew that the idea was a wild one. But this was his one chance to be free—free of Ah Gow and prison.

The boy quickly took off his jacket and dived over the rail. Down, down, down he went, into the cold water. At last he came up again. He filled his lungs with air and looked about. He saw the face of Ah Gow above him.

"Fool, fool!" cried Ah Gow.

Yat Sang turned and looked toward the bamboo sails. Then he started swimming. The water was as cold as ice. The strong current kept pulling him back. The longer he swam, the farther away the bamboo sails seemed to be.

The young swimmer rested a moment. Then he raised his arm and yelled. He did not know whether the fishermen heard him. Even as he rested, the current was pulling him away from the junk. He was tired now. Salt water filled his mouth and nose.

The boy swam on and on. Then he heard the shouts of the fishermen. At last he felt strong arms pulling him to safety. It was the last thing he remembered.

2

Smoke! Sweet-smelling tea! Fish! Boiling rice! Yat Sang sniffed the well-known odors. Then he opened his eyes. He was lying on a bunk in a tiny hut. There were many bunks around the walls. The fishermen were warming their hands over a small stove in the corner.

Yat Sang sat up slowly. His eyes rested on a small wooden figure on a shelf. It was Ma Chu, the goddess of sailors. No fisherman's home was ever without a figure of Ma Chu. She watched over all men of the sea. She kept them safe from the terrible Sea Dragon, who ruled the waters.

Yat Sang smiled. "Thank you, Ma Chu," he whispered.

One of the fishermen turned. "Look!" the man said. "Our big fish has opened his eyes."

The captain brought bowls of tea and rice. "What were you trying to do—swim back to China?" he asked. "You were nearly dead when we picked you up. But eat now. Your story can wait."

It seemed to Yat Sang that his stomach had been empty for months. It was hard not to make a pig of himself. But he ate each mouthful slowly and politely. When he had finished, he began his story:

"I lived on the great river of China, on my father's junk. There were seven in my family. We were very poor. Often we did not have enough to eat."

The fishermen nodded. They had lived in much the same way.

"Then the great floods came," Yat Sang went on. "My father's junk was broken to bits. The times that followed were very bad. My sisters were sold as slaves. It was then that I began to think of America."

"But how did you find money to pay your fare?" the captain asked.

Yat Sang shook his head. "I wasn't able to get the money. Agents were hiring men for jobs in America. The men's fares were paid by American companies. But the agents were looking for men—not boys. They only laughed at me. They wouldn't hire me."

"You have done a man's work if you lived on a river boat," said one of the fishermen.

"So I told the agents," said Yat Sang. "But they didn't believe me. And, because I owned nothing, no one would lend me money for my fare. One day I went to the docks. I saw an American ship making ready to leave. I thought of my family, poor and hungry. I thought of the rich land across the water, where jobs were easy to find."

"And so you hid aboard the ship?" asked the captain, smiling.

Yat Sang nodded. Then he told the men about Ah Gow, who had said that Yat Sang would be put into prison.

"Ah Gow was lying," the captain said. "You could have gone to the Hop Wo Company, or one of the others. There are many Chinese here. We help one another.

"If I had only known that!" Yat Sang cried. "I'd have saved myself a swim. But I'm here. That is the important thing. Now I must find work, so that I can send money to my family. And I must pay the money for my fare. That must be done before the New Year."

The captain said, "The Americans don't feel about the New Year as we Chinese do. You may pay the steamship company any time you wish."

Yat Sang cried, "But I am Chinese, not American! I must pay my debt before the New Year! It is the way of our people. It is a matter of honor."

The captain nodded. "Yes, you're right. We should follow the ways of our people, even in this new land."

There was much that Yat Sang wanted to know

about the new land. Was there gold to be found in its hills? Could a man here really become rich in a few years? Were the stories that he had heard in China true?

The fishermen looked at one another. At first they did not answer. Then one spoke up. "There are no more Chinese in the gold mines. The Americans don't want us to take their gold. But there are other jobs. Some of them pay as much as a dollar a day."

Again the men were silent for a moment. Then the captain said slowly. "Some Americans are kind. Some are not. Some are wise, and others are very stupid. Stay close to your own people. Stay out of trouble's way. It is easier."

"Tell the boy the truth. He'll soon learn it anyway," said one of the men in a hard voice. "They neither like nor want us. To the Americans, you and I are less than nothing."

Later, Yat Sang lay on his narrow bunk, thinking of all that the men had said. Ayah! It would not be easy for him in this strange land. It would be still harder to be unwanted. With all his heart, the boy longed to be back on the great river of China. He had known fear there, and hunger, too. True, he had seen the angry waters tear his home to bits. But at least the dangers were well-known dangers. But here—who knew?

3

Yat Sang could not wait for a first look at his new home. He walked carefully over the broken boxes and old jars. There were squash vines everywhere. Their yellow flowers were the only spots of color in the whole place. Everything else looked gray in the early light. Even the hills and the fog over the water were gray. The mud flats were gray-brown. So were the tiny huts, made of rotting boards and standing above the water on long, slim poles.

"What do you think of our camp?" Yat Sang heard someone ask. He turned to find the captain coming up the hill behind him.

Yat Sang smiled and said, "I think I'm going to like it."

"We have food and a roof over our heads," said the captain. "It is enough for now. We left China, poor men. But in a year—two years, perhaps—we'll return as rich men. Ayah! At home, it would take three lifetimes of hard work to become as rich as we'll be."

"Is there work that I can do here at the camp?" asked Yat Sang.

The captain nodded and said, "Men are always coming and going. There is always room for one more. But we won't fish today. There is other work to do. In a few days, we'll go after shrimp. The nets must be ready. And we must take our dried fish to the city—perhaps tomorrow."

All day Yat Sang worked beside the fishermen. They filled every basket with fish and abalone shells. Then they made a place on the hillside to dry the shrimp. They cut down the weeds and swept the place smooth. At sundown, they started back to their hut.

"You've done a man's work today, Yat Sang," said the captain. "When we sell our fish, you'll have some of the money we get."

Yat Sang smiled and said, "I'm a step closer to paying my debt. I'll soon have money to send to my family. Tell me, who buys our fish and shrimp? The Americans?"

The captain shook his head. "They buy only our abalone shells for jewelry," he answered. "The Americans don't like our dried fish and dried shrimp. Our tea farmers in China use the shells around their plants."

Yat Sang was tired after his day in the sun. He went to sleep after his supper of rice and tea. It seemed that he had hardly closed his eyes when the captain wakened him.

"What! Is it morning already?" the boy asked. He

sat up and rubbed his eyes. He was still so sleepy and tired he could hardly think.

"It is sunrise—the Hour of the Tiger," said the captain. "We must be on our way to the city."

After a cup of tea, Yat Sang followed the fishermen to the hill. They hung each basket on a long pole, which two men carried between them. They started for the city, trotting along the hill. The baskets between them swung at every step.

It was still dark when the party left the camp. But, by the time they reached the city, the sun was high in the sky. Yat Sang saw booths and stalls in every alley and doorway. The shops were full of Chinese foods and Chinese goods. Charcoal smoke came from every window. Washing hung from the roof tops, and from lines high above the street.

"But this is like a Chinese city!" said Yat Sang, surprised. "I had thought that America would be very different."

The captain smiled. "It is different," he said. "But, here in Chinatown, our people live in our own way. Our gods and our customs are thousands of years old. We do not leave them behind when we leave China."

Yat Sang looked at the signs on the doors they passed. Here was a joss house, home of all the Chinese gods of old. Inside, a priest was banging on a large metal gong. The noise was expected to waken

the sleeping gods. Then the gods would listen to the prayers of those who came to ask for help.

The fishermen and Yat Sang passed the house of the Sacred Fires. Every paper with Chinese writing on it was sacred—no matter how small the scrap of paper was. Such papers would be burned in the Sacred Fires. Then the ashes would be taken out to sea and thrown upon the waters.

Yat Sang was so busy looking around that he fell behind the others. They were soon out of sight. Where had they turned off? There were so many narrow, dark alleys that Yat Sang did not know where to look.

The street was filled with Chinese. All of them wore blue cotton jackets and flat straw hats. Yat Sang looked everywhere for the captain's red head cloth.

Suddenly, the lost boy saw a face that filled him with fear. "Ah Gow!" he said to himself.

The agent was coming toward Yat Sang. The boy ducked into a doorway. He stood there, holding his breath and afraid to move. Had he been seen? The fishermen had said that he need not fear Ah Gow. But they did not know the man. As long as Ah Gow knew about Yat Sang's unpaid debt, he had the power to harm the boy.

"Ah Gow mustn't find me now," thought Yat Sang. "Not yet—not until my debt is paid."

The boy waited in the doorway until Ah Gow had passed. But his knees were still shaking. And Chinatown had lost its friendly look.

"Ayah! I have no money," he said to himself. "If I can't find my friends, I'll lose my share for the work I did."

Worst of all, Yat Sang knew that he might meet Ah Gow again at any minute. He started to walk, not knowing where he was going. The streets and buildings began to look strange to him. He saw no more Chinese faces. He was in the American part of the city now, and he was afraid.

Suddenly, Yat Sang heard men shouting. He could not understand what they said. He stopped in the middle of the street, wondering what the noise was about. He heard the sound of wheels and pounding hoofs. Then he turned. He had only started to run when a horse-drawn carriage hit him.

4

When Yat Sang awoke, two strangers stood beside him. One was an old Chinese. The other was an American. The American's curly black beard made his face look stern. But his eyes were kind.

"Where am I? What happened?" Yat Sang asked, trying to sit up. As he moved, a sharp pain shot up his arm. He lay back on the bed and looked about the strange room.

"Don't be afraid," said the old Chinese, seeing the fear in the boy's eyes. "You're in Mr. Kelly's home. You were hit by his horses when they ran away with the carriage. He brought you here. You are, indeed, lucky. Another man might have left you in the street."

Yat Sang nodded. "Ayah!" he said. "It is so. Do you work here?"

"Yes," answered the Chinese. "I have taken care of this family for many years."

Mr. Kelly stood up. "I think the boy is going to be all right, Lee," he said to the old man. "Please tell him how sorry I am, and take good care of him."

The door closed behind Mr. Kelly. Lee picked up a small white bowl. "Your arm is broken and must be taken care of," he said. "See, I have mixed clay with the blood of a chicken. Now I'll put it on your arm."

While Lee talked, his fingers were busy. He covered the clay with strips of cloth and thin bamboo. Then he put more chicken blood over the bamboo.

When the job was done, Yat Sang thanked Lee. "How long will it take the arm to mend?" the worried boy asked. "I am new in this country. I must find work soon."

"It won't take long," Lee told Yat Sang. "If you want a job, why not stay here? It would pay you ten dollars a month—more, if you learn quickly and work hard. In a few years, I'll go back to China. Then you could take my place. You'd make thirty dollars a month then."

"Until my arm mends, I can't look for other work," thought Yat Sang. "And, if I went back to Chinatown, I'd be seeing Ah Gow again!"

"Rest now," Lee said. "We'll talk of the work another time."

In the days that followed, Yat Sang found himself wanting to stay with the Kellys. More and more, he hated the thought of leaving them. They were a kind and happy family—Mr. and Mrs. Kelly and young David, their son. But Yat Sang knew that he would soon need more money. He had already sent a small sum to his family in China. He was saving the rest of his money to pay his debt. Even so, his savings were growing too slowly. He knew that he would not have the fifty-four dollars he needed when the New Year came.

Yat Sang started many times to say something to Lee about leaving. But something happened to stop him every time. Sometimes it was a picnic or a trip. At other times, it was nothing more than a smile from Mrs. Kelly. When she smiled at him, the boy's heart would turn over, and he would say nothing.

One day David ran into the kitchen. He was very excited. He whispered to Lee a long time. Yat Sang could not understand what they were saying. But he felt sure that the secret had to do with him.

"What's going on?" Yat Sang asked Lee.

Lee only smiled and said, "I can't tell. It's David's secret. But you'll find out when winter comes. It's of great importance to you."

That night Yat Sang counted his money again. "It won't be enough," he said to himself sadly. "But I must wait until I find out about the secret."

Yat Sang was soon too busy to think of either money or the secret. The Kellys were leaving for their ranch in the valley.

"There's much to be done before we go," Lee told him. "You're to help Mrs. Kelly clean the house. I must fill the baskets with food for our trip. We'll go by boat, across the bay and up the river."

After two busy days, the family was ready to go. Early in the morning, they drove down to the dock. Lee and Yat Sang rode on the back of the carriage. As the carriage bumped over the rough streets, they hung on for dear life.

5

The Kelly ranch was a big one. Fields of green and purple grapes reached as far as eye could see. Chinese pickers were already at work in the fields. At sundown they left the fields and went to their camp.

Yat Sang hurried through his work at the ranch house. He looked longingly at the pickers' camp. It was an old building, with a kitchen and bunk rooms. Beside the building was an open lean-to, with a brush roof. The men gathered here in the cool of the evening. Yat Sang could hear their talk and laughter coming up the hill.

"May I go down to the camp for a while?" the boy asked Lee.

"Wait, and I'll go with you," Lee said. "I think you've been lonely. You spend too many nights in your room at the Kellys'. You should go to Chinatown every night, as I do."

The little room was lonely. Yat Sang had never before slept in a room by himself. In China, there were always many people around. Families were large, and homes were crowded. In Chinatown, too, men lived together, as they did in the Old Country.

"Perhaps I'll go with you sometime," Yat Sang

said. But he knew that he could not do that until his debt had been paid. If he did, he might run into Ah Gow.

Lee and Yat Sang had reached the camp. Yat Sang saw a small altar in the lean-to. Punk sticks were burning before it. They were stuck in old jars and in pieces of melon rind. The Chinese burn punk sticks in their places of worship, as we burn candles in many of ours.

Lee met an old friend. "But I didn't expect to see you here," Lee said to his friend. "I thought you were in the mountains, working on the railroad."

"And so I was—for a time," the friend said. "But that's no place for an old man—nor for a young one, either. The work is dangerous. If you don't freeze to death, you're hit by falling rocks. One day half the mountain came sliding down on us. I saw five men trapped. When we dug them out—Ayah! They

were flatter than pressed ducks!" The old man shook his head sadly.

Yat Sang listened to the men around him for a long time. He was happy to be among his own people again. They talked of life in the California mines before the Chinese had been driven out. They talked of their work in the fishing camps. They spoke of the railroad, the streets, the roads, and the cities that they were helping to build. These men had worked at many jobs in many places. They spoke, too, of their families in China. Yat Sang saw the longing in their eyes as they talked of home.

Yat Sang went to the pickers' camp every night. Finally the harvest was over, and the pickers left. It was time for the Kellys to return to the city. They went back, as they had come—on a river boat.

All the way, Yat Sang and David hung over the rail. They watched the golden fields moving by. Down the river and across the bay they went. Now the paddle wheel turned more slowly. The boat was coming near the dock.

"Let's watch the sailors tie up the boat," David called. Yat Sang did not understand, but he followed his friend along the deck. David ran ahead.

Suddenly, Yat Sang cried out. But his warning came too late. David had not seen the coil of rope on the boat. The rope was like a great snake. It

wound around David's feet and jerked him overboard.

Men yelled. Yat Sang reached the rail in time to see David's red hair sinking under the dark water. Over he went, after his friend. Yat Sang dived once—twice. The third time, he found David. He quickly tore the rope from the boy's leg and pulled him up. He swam for the dock.

It seemed forever that the men were working over David. Water poured from the boy's mouth and nose. Yat Sang could not take his eyes from David's white face.

"He must not die!" Yat Sang said over and over to himself. "He must live! He must live!"

At last David began to gasp. The worst was over. David was alive. Mr. Kelly wrapped his son in his coat and held him close. Mrs. Kelly put her hands over her face. Her knees seemed to give way. Had Yat Sang not rushed to her side, she would have fallen.

"Oh, Yat Sang," sobbed Mrs. Kelly, holding him tightly. "God bless you for saving my son."

Yat Sang's ears did not know what Mrs. Kelly's words meant. But his heart understood them.

6

Yat Sang put his few belongings together. He tied them up into a small bundle. He took one last look around his room. Then he went down to the kitchen.

"Where are you going?" Lee asked in surprise. "There's work to be done."

"I'm leaving," Yat Sang told Lee. "I'm going to look for another job."

"But you have a job!" Lee's voice was high and excited. "You can't go now. There's the secret—David's secret to think of. Yat Sang, you don't know what you'll miss if you leave here now."

"I don't want to go," Yat Sang said. "But I have thought about it for many months. There is no other way for me. I can't wait for the surprise." Then Yat Sang told Lee the story of his debt.

"But I have money," Lee told him. "I'll help you pay the debt. Then you can stay here."

"But you are saving your money to go home," Yat Sang cried. "I wouldn't take it from you."

Mr. Kelly heard their excited voices. He came into the kitchen. "What's the trouble?" he asked Lee.

Mr. Kelly and Lee talked for a long time. Yat Sang looked from one to the other, wishing that he could understand their words.

Then Lee turned to Yat Sang. "Mr. Kelly wants to know the name of the ship that brought you to California," the old man said.

The boy shook his head. "I don't know that," he said.

Lee threw up his hands. "You don't know the ship company. The ship company doesn't know you. What does it matter whether you pay, or don't pay? This is all foolishness."

"But I know that I owe the money," said Yat Sang quietly. "I must pay. It's a debt of honor."

Lee sighed and wiped his hands on his apron. Then he turned to Mr. Kelly, and they talked together again. At last Mr. Kelly left the room.

Lee said, "Everything will be taken care of. Now put down your bundle and get about your work. Mr. Kelly will pay the ship company. He'll bring you a slip of paper, showing that the debt has been paid."

"But—but—," said Yat Sang. He could not believe his ears.

"You may as well know the rest, too," Lee said. "David's teacher will come in a few days. You're to learn to speak English, and to read and write it, too. That was David's secret. And there's one more thing. When you've learned to speak English, you're to go to Mr. Kelly. There's something he wants to tell you then. It's very important."

Yat Sang went about his work, feeling as though he were dreaming. He had never dared to wish for anything so wonderful. To think of learning to read and write! To be able to talk to his American friends! In China, anyone who could read and write was an important person. But a poor river-boat boy worked from sun to sun. He had no time for lessons.

Yat Sang worked hard at his lessons. He learned quickly. Christmas passed, and the American New Year's Day. Then it was time for the Chinese New Year.

"We'll have a whole week off for our New Year!" Lee told Yat Sang. Surely, you'll want to spend that week among our own people. Come with me to Chinatown."

Yat Sang smiled. His debt was paid. He no longer had to fear Ah Gow. "Yes, I'll go with you," he said. "But I have something important to do first."

Yat Sang hurried to find Mr. Kelly. "Sir, I have learned English. Lee said that you wanted to speak to me when I had."

Mr. Kelly nodded. "I've been waiting for this day, Yat Sang," he said. "What I have to tell you, I must say in my own words. But for you, my only son would be dead. You gave him the chance to live." Mr. Kelly leaned forward in his chair. "There are no words in any tongue to thank you for that. I could give you money, but money would soon be gone. If I could, I'd rather give you a chance for a better life, Yat Sang. What kind of work would you really like to do when you grow up?"

The boy shook his head slowly. "Why—why, I hadn't thought of it," he said. "I don't know. A poor person thinks only of staying alive from day to day."

Mr. Kelly smiled. "Of course. But you must think beyond that now. You must choose a life work someday. Mrs. Kelly and I will see that you have whatever schooling you'll need for that. We want to do for you just as we'll do for our own son."

The gift of learning—the gift of a new life! How did one give thanks for such things? Yat Sang was silent.

"You have plenty of time to think it over," Mr. Kelly said, smiling. "Now go along with Lee. I hope you'll both have a happy New Year."

The New Year festival was always gay and exciting. But there had never been one like this! Yat Sang went through the week as though he were walking on clouds. Firecrackers were popping all around him. Every shop was filled with good things. Sweet-smelling China lilies bloomed everywhere in Chinatown. Crowds of happy people filled the streets. There was a great parade. A make-believe dragon went down the street, followed by figures of all the Chinese gods.

At last the holiday was over. Yat Sang started up the hill. His arms were full of gifts for the Kellys—a pot of lilies, lichee nuts, ginger, and salted fruits. Suddenly, he saw a well-known face among the crowd of people. It was Ah Gow! The boy called out a greeting.

Ah Gow stopped. He looked poor and shabby. "You?" he said, his mouth dropping open. "But I didn't think I'd ever see you alive again."

"I'm very much alive, thank you," said Yat Sang. "And I've also paid my debt to the steamship company. I have a piece of paper to prove it."

Ah Gow had not lost his sly grin. "Indeed," he said. "You must have done well here." Ah Gow's narrow eyes took in Yat Sang's new cotton suit and the red ribbon in his queue. "What will you do now?" he added. "Return to China?"

"No," Yat Sang said slowly. "No. I'm going home."

Something strange and wonderful had happened to Yat Sang. In his heart he knew it as he answered

Ah Gow. He was no longer a stranger in a strange land!

"It's true," he said to himself. "I am going home."

Smiling, the boy from China trotted off to his American family, his arms full of gifts.

Pioneers from Europe

THE people of Europe had long looked westward to America. Here was a land where they could hope for a better life. Throughout the years, people had come from many countries of Europe to settle in the United States. America was a young, growing nation and needed their strong arms. Thousands came each year to find work and a better life in America.

Covered-wagon days were gone forever. Westward travel was easy now. The railroad brought thousands of families to California's cities and valleys. Among them were many Italians. They found the state's sunny hills much like the hills of their old homeland. They planted orchards and vineyards. They helped to build California's fruit and fishing industries. They brought their art of wine making—and a new industry was born in California.

"Stranger at Cherry Hill" tells of an Italian family who came to California in 1890.

STRANGER AT CHERRY HILL

1

It was payday! Domenic had been in America a year. But he still could not get over the wonder of payday. And this payday was an important one! This time Domenic might get the ball and bat he longed for. If only he could make Papa see how badly he needed them!

Dina, Domenic's older sister, helped him to clear the dishes from the table. The Bertoli house did not have a sink in the kitchen. The children piled the dishes in a big tin dishpan on the worktable. An old iron teakettle had been hissing on the back of the wood stove. Domenic took it up and poured some boiling water over the dishes.

"Shall I fill the kettle and the wood box now—or later?" he asked.

"Oh, later, later," Papa said. "Leave the dishes. Come and sit down, all of you."

"Work is for peasants, eh?" Mama said, laughing. "Tonight we are so rich that we'll leave the dishes to soak." She brushed the last crumb from the oilcloth that covered the pine table. She wiped her hands on her apron and sat down by Papa.

Dina and Dom slid into their places. An oil lamp hung over the table. It threw a warm light on the four faces.

Papa leaned back in his chair. His stomach was full of good food. His pockets were full of money. The spring garden was finished. The whole family had worked until dark, setting out the last of the tomato plants. The plants would surely bear a lot of fine tomatoes. They had been set out during the first days of the new moon. Yes, Papa felt good tonight. He wiped his mustache and lighted his pipe. He moved the wine jug from the center of the table.

"Now is everyone ready?" he asked. "Dom, you look ready to burst. I think we'll hear from you first."

Domenic pushed his money to the center of the table. "This has been the best month of all," he said proudly.

Dina opened her eyes wide. "You surely didn't make all that from milk and eggs," she said. "You must have found a gold mine."

Domenic nodded. "You will never guess where—in the town dump! You should see what is thrown away there. I have done well, just selling empty bottles."

Mama rented rooms to three young Italians who worked with Papa on the railroad. She added her rent money to Domenic's. Dina worked part time at the hotel. She also did washing and ironing for Mama's roomers. She slid her earnings across the table.

Last of all, Papa emptied his pockets. With his month's pay from the railroad company, the pile of money looked like a mountain to Domenic. In Italy, there had never been such a thing as a payday

157

for the Bertolis. They had raised their crops on land that belonged to another family. They had kept only a small part of the crop for themselves. No matter how hard they worked, they had barely earned their daily bread—nothing more, ever.

In California, they worked just as hard. But things were different here. Each month the Bertolis had something to show for their work. They even had some money left over, to save in their little tin box. Papa Bertoli was already a *padrone*—a landowner! He had come to California first and had worked and saved. He had bought land and a house before he had sent to Italy for his family. During the last year, the family had built a new barn. Now they had a cow and a calf in the barn, two horses, and a fine wagon. They had chickens and rabbits, too. Think of it! Meat, eggs, and butter every day. The Bertolis could hardly believe that they had become so rich.

Domenic sat still, his chin in his hands. He watched his father divide the money into smaller piles.

"Here is money for the flour and *pasta* we will have to buy, Mama. We'll lay this aside to buy the pig we want. And this is for lumber to build a pen for the pig." Papa Bertoli looked around. "Now who needs shoes? Clothing? Speak up!"

Domenic wet his lips with his tongue. The time

had come. "I need a ball and bat, please, Papa." The boy's voice was low, but firm.

"A which?" his father asked, frowning.

"A ball and bat—for baseball. It's a game the boys play at school. If I could learn to pitch and hit well enough, I could be on the school team. Everybody plays, and it's important. It's really important—."

Domenic stopped. Three pairs of brown eyes were staring at him. It was plain that not one of the family knew what he was talking about. And there were no Italian words to tell them.

"Basa-ball—basa-ball? What kind of thing is that?" Papa asked. "You mean they teach games at school? You *play?* You do not read and write?" Papa turned to Mama. "I come halfway round the world so my son can have a good education, a chance in life. And what does he do? Plays the basa-ball."

"Oh, we work hard, too. We study," Domenic said quickly. It was hard to tell Papa anything when he was excited. "But, you see, it is different here. Baseball is important. You just have to believe me. I can't tell you how it is."

The boy swallowed hard. He *had* to have that ball and bat! It meant everything to him. He had to be a good player! If he could make the baseball team, things might be different for him. The other boys might look up to him. He could make friends.

He could be "somebody," just as Will Todd was "somebody."

Papa rubbed his mustache. "Well, I don't know," he said. "Mama, what do you say?"

Mama's face was troubled. In the Old Country, everything had been no, no, no. There was more money now. But the Bertolis were still plain, working people. They were not rich. It would not do for Domenic to get too many fancy ideas, like this basaball. Still, if his marks were good, and his work was done—.

"I think—yes. Yes," Mama finally said.

Dina nodded her head. And at last Papa nodded, too. Domenic sighed with relief. It was over.

That night the boy could hardly sleep for thinking of the ball and bat. The big game of the year was not far off. Cherry Hill School would soon play against the team from Watertown. If only he could play in that game! He would show them!

Domenic smiled as he fell asleep. He dreamed that Domenic Bertoli was making home run after home run. In his dream he saw Will Todd shaking his hand. He seemed to hear everyone from Cherry Hill shouting, "Hurrah for Dom!"

But even as he dreamed, Domenic knew that the dream was wrong. No one at school called him "Dom" in the old, friendly way. He was "Domenic Bertoli—that Italian boy."

2

Cherry Hill's main street was only a block long. The sidewalks were made of rough boards. The wooden buildings had once been painted white. But now they were as colorless as the dusty street. Domenic hurried down a narrow alley. He passed behind the hotel where Dina worked. He passed the livery stable, with its buggies and nodding horses. One buggy was always kept there for Doctor Todd, who very often had a rush call to make.

The blacksmith shop came next. Gus, the blacksmith, was working the bellows. "Hello, Domenic," he called. "You are early this morning."

Domenic smiled and waved. "I'd like to stop and

talk with you, but Mrs. Todd wants her eggs and milk before breakfast," he said.

The boy hurried past Mr. Wilson's grocery store. When Papa grew more food than the family needed, he traded it to Mr. Wilson for other things. At last Domenic went through the back gate of the big, white house on the corner. Dr. Todd's house was the only building on the block with a fresh coat of paint. Domenic left his milk and eggs inside the doctor's screen porch.

Mrs. Todd waved and smiled from the kitchen window. Sometimes she asked the boy in and gave

him a freshly baked sweet roll. Domenic walked slowly to the gate, hoping that he would be called back. But Mrs. Todd did not call him this morning. He went on to school.

The schoolyard was fenced all around to keep out the cattle. Domenic climbed the stile and went up the boardwalk of the building. The school, too, needed a new coat of paint. Its high windows looked dark and empty. The bell would not ring for nearly an hour yet. Domenic was always the first one to get to school.

The boy batted rocks with a stick. "I am getting better at this," he said to himself. "By Saturday, I'll have my new ball and bat."

Suddenly, he heard a sound, as though a window had been closed. The sound came from behind the school. Domenic frowned. Who else could be here so early? He started around the side of the building to see where the noise had come from.

At the corner, he met Porky Lester. Domenic stopped. He took a step backward. "Oh, hello, Porky," he said, in surprise.

Porky grabbed Domenic and pinned him to the wall. "What are you snooping around for?" Porky asked angrily.

"Why, nothing. I—." Porky had such a tight hold on his collar that Domenic could hardly talk.

Porky was the biggest boy in the whole class, and the meanest. The other children were not very friendly. But they at least left Domenic alone.

Porky pressed his fat, red face against Domenic's. "You never saw *nobody,* and you never saw *noth-*

ing," he said slowly. "And don't you forget it, see? Or I'll get you for sure." He gave Domenic a push, and walked off. In a moment, Porky was gone.

Domenic rubbed his neck. What had Porky been up to? Whatever it was, Domenic wanted nothing to do with it. He hurried away from the building. He climbed the front fence and waited for the other pupils.

The other children came by twos and threes, swinging the lard pails that held their lunches. Those from the village of Cherry Hill came on foot. Those from the farms came on horseback. The two Jensen boys were coming down the road now. Each day Domenic wondered whether their bony old horse would ever reach the school. It seemed about to die on its feet.

Domenic looked down at his overalls. He tried to smooth his hair. Every morning he held his head under the pump and tried to make his wet hair lie flat. But he could never look like those Jensen boys, with their neat suits and slick yellow hair.

Miss Gray, the teacher, walked into the yard with Will and Jenny Todd. She lived at the Todds' big white house. She lifted her long, full skirt and started up the school steps. Domenic jumped from the fence. He ran to join the others, and they lined up behind Miss Gray.

The teacher unlocked the door and reached for the bell rope. Then suddenly she jumped back. A fat skunk came flying out of the door, his bushy tail waving. The children screamed and jumped out of its path.

"Porky Lester!" Domenic thought. "So *that* was his trick."

"Help me open all the windows, Will," said Miss Gray. "Jenny, run home and bring me a pan of vinegar. We'll boil it on the stove. It will help to get rid of this terrible odor."

Miss Gray sent Domenic and two of the bigger boys to the woodshed. They were to fill the wood box, then start a fire in the black iron stove. The smell of the skunk was bad, and the odor from the boiling vinegar helped little.

"We'll have our lessons on the front steps during the first hour," Miss Gray said. Her face was almost white. Her blue eyes were angry. "And now I want to know who put that skunk in the room."

No one said a word. Domenic saw Porky shaking a fist at him. "All right," said Miss Gray. "If the one who did it won't tell the truth, I'll have to punish you all. We'll play no more baseball until I find out who brought that skunk to school."

"What about our game with Watertown?" Will spoke up.

"No more baseball," Miss Gray said. Her mouth was set in a thin line.

The boys groaned. Domenic heard two girls whispering behind him.

"I'll bet I know who did it," one said. "It was that Domenic Bertoli. He's always the first one at school."

The whisper was passed from one pupil to the other. Soon, twenty pairs of eyes were looking angrily at Domenic.

3

Each day was a little worse for Domenic. He had his new ball and bat. But what was the use now? If he were the best player in the world, the other boys would never let him be on the team.

The big game with Watertown was to be played on Friday. Porky Lester still had not told Miss Gray about the skunk. He was happy to let everyone think that Domenic had played the trick on her. The last few days Porky had come to school with a dirty rag around one hand. His hand was badly swollen. Porky said that he had cut it.

"You *have* to tell, Porky," Domenic told him.

"Why should I?" Porky asked. "I'm not on the team. Neither are you. Who cares about their old game anyway? You keep still, do you hear?"

"I *won't* keep still!" Domenic said angrily. "If you don't tell, I will. I'm not going to let Cherry Hill miss the big game."

"Ha! Who would believe you? You're not even an American. You say *one word,* and you know what I'll do? I'll say that I saw you bringing the skunk to school." Porky walked off, his hands in his pockets.

Domenic looked after him, his heart sinking. Every word that Porky had said was true. He was a stranger. No one trusted him. What good would it do to tell on Porky?

It was lunchtime. As always, the class formed a line and marched out the front door. The Jensen boys ran to their horse, carrying it a nose bag full of oats. The girls lined up on the top steps with their lunch pails. They tossed their pigtails and talked and laughed. Each of them wore long, black cotton stockings. Their high voices and skinny legs made Domenic think of blackbirds on a fence.

Porky began the old game. "I see an old dead rat," he shouted.

"I one it," one of the other boys piped up. "I two it. I three it. I four it," the rest joined in.

"I seven it," Porky said. "Come on, Domenic. You're next. What comes after seven?"

"Eight?" Domenic asked, wondering what this was all about. "I—eight it?"

"Ho! Ho! Domenic ate a dead rat," Porky shouted. "Hey, you don't want that old dead rat, do you?" He knocked Domenic's sandwich from his hand. The good bread, the salami, and the cheese rolled into the dirt.

Will Todd stood up. "Oh, cut it out, Porky," he said. "Let Domenic alone."

Another boy said, "Why stick up for him? He won't even own up and tell the truth. If we don't get to play Watertown, it'll be his fault."

"Well, it's not for you to punish him," Will said quietly.

The others were silent. Will was a tall, quiet boy. He was well liked. Domenic looked up at Will, wanting to thank him. But Will looked away.

Friday morning came. As always, Domenic hurried to the Todd house with his milk and eggs. Will was waiting for him on the screen porch.

"Listen, Domenic," he said. "For the last five years, Watertown has won every game from us. This is the first year we've had a good team. We could win that game tonight if we just had the chance. If you put that skunk in the room, won't you please tell Miss Gray? We don't want to miss the biggest game of the year."

"But, I—." Domenic stopped. What was the use? It was as Porky had said. Nobody believed him—not even Will. Domenic turned and walked slowly through the gate. His heart was like a cold, heavy stone.

The unhappy boy cut through the old orchard and headed for school. The orchard did not belong to anyone. The trees were not taken care of. The fruit lay on the ground to rot. Domenic had been surprised the first time he had seen it there. In his homeland, not an inch of land was wasted. The farmer slept with one eye open, lest someone make off with an egg or a bunch of grapes. The olives were counted on the trees. It was not easy to make a living from Italy's stony hills. But here, in America, there was food to throw away. Rich, rich America!

Rich, yes. But so lonely for Domenic! At school, the others looked at him and turned away. He kept his head down, trying not to hear the whispers. Miss Gray rapped on her desk with her pencil.

"Does anyone care to tell us about the skunk? If not, there will be no game this afternoon," she said.

No one spoke. Domenic looked at Porky Lester's seat. It was empty!

Slowly, Domenic stood up. Every eye was on him. All the others were waiting—waiting for him to speak. "I did it," he heard himself say. What difference did it make? They wanted to believe the lie. They did not like him. If they missed the game, it would only be worse for him.

In Italy, the schoolmaster punished the children by making them kneel on grains of corn. Miss Gray used a willow rod. The whipping was soon over, and Domenic was glad.

4

It was Sunday. Domenic was sitting with his father under the fig tree in the backyard. They could hear Dina and Mama Bertoli singing in the kitchen. Good smells of spice and garlic came from the open window.

"Get the ball and bat, Dom," his father said. "Let's see how this basa-ball thing works."

Domenic shook his head. "Oh, it's too hot. Later, maybe."

Papa Bertoli looked at his son. "What's the matter with you? You go around looking like a sick dog all the time. Is something wrong?"

"No. Nothing is wrong," Domenic said slowly. He wanted to tell his father the truth. But it would only worry him. Papa could do nothing to help anyhow. He was a stranger to American ways—even more of a stranger than Domenic, who went to an American school. Papa still had his Old Country ideas, and his few Italian friends.

"I've been thinking, Papa," Domenic said. "I had three years of school in Italy, and I've had a year here. Maybe it is time that I quit and went to work."

Papa looked hurt and surprised. "Don't think of such a thing!" he said. "In Italy, maybe you'd have quit school and gone to work. But not here! No, no! You finish school, you hear? You have a big chance here—a big chance."

Domenic swallowed hard. He could not hurt his father. He would have to go back to Cherry Hill. There was no way out.

Mama called from the kitchen window, "Have you two forgotten that company is coming to dinner? Come on, get busy. They'll be here soon, and the table isn't ready."

Papa brought long boards and sawhorses and made a table under the grape arbor. Domenic brought chairs from the house. Dina covered the boards with oilcloth and set the plates around.

"I hear the wagon now," Domenic said. He and his father hurried to the front yard. A wagon was rattling down the road, pulled by a pair of horses.

Papa hitched the horses to the post while Dom helped to lift the smaller children from the wagon. The older children jumped over the side. There were three families to unload. Nearly every Sunday they drove the long way to Cherry Hill for a visit.

"Hello, Dom."
"How is everyone?"
"How is school?"
"Where are Mama and Dina?"

Dom grinned and shook his head. There was no

way to answer everyone at once. The women were soon running up and down the steps, bringing food from the kitchen. There were bowls of salted olives. There were olives in oil, with garlic and herbs. There were hot peppers and sweet peppers, carrots and radishes—all from Papa's garden. There were good cheeses, and lots of dry salami. There were stacks of Mama's crusty bread that had been baked in the outdoor oven. And this was only the beginning. Afterward came the *pasta*—spaghetti and ravioli. Then came pork and chicken, each in its spicy gravy. And, for anyone who might still be hungry, there was fresh fruit on the table.

After dinner, the older folks sat under the cool arbor, joking and laughing. The children played. Domenic joined them, but his heart was not in their games. He could think of nothing but school and the lonely days ahead.

On Monday morning, Domenic left his milk and eggs at the Todd house. Then he went back down the alley to see Gus, the blacksmith. He did not want to be the first one at school ever again.

"Hello, hello," Gus greeted him. "So you have time for a little visit this morning, eh? Good!"

Gus liked visitors. The men in the village gathered at his shop to talk and to watch him work. Gus knew everything that happened in Cherry Hill.

"You see the big ball game Friday afternoon, Dom?" he asked. "They say it was a close one."

Domenic shook his head. "No, I—I couldn't make it. Who won?"

"Cherry Hill won," Gus answered. "The first time in five years, they tell me. Give me a hand with this plow, will you, son? Jake Lester will be wanting it back by noon today. Say, you heard about Porky, didn't you?"

"About Porky?" Domenic asked. "What happened to him?"

"Oh, my! He's bad off, he is. His Pa says they took

him to the hospital in town. Blood poisoning. Skunk bit him on the hand awhile back. Doc Todd says they just barely saved his arm."

So that was why Porky had kept his hand covered! And all the time, he had been afraid to tell about the skunk bite. But the truth was out now. Since Doctor Todd knew about Porky, Will and Jenny would know, too. And so would Miss Gray.

Domenic picked up his lunch pail. "Guess I'll be on my way, Gus," he said. "Thanks for all the news."

"Sure, sure. Don't you be late for school. And listen, Dom, don't let anybody tell you you're not American, see? All of us came from another country, or our folks did." The blacksmith grinned. "Old Gus knows. He hears things. Now, go along with you, and remember what I said."

Domenic raced through the old orchard and up the dusty road. He grinned when he saw his teacher.

"Good morning, Miss Gray," he called.

Miss Gray stopped him. "Wait, Domenic. I want to talk with you," she said. "Why did you let me whip you for something another boy had done?"

Domenic looked at his feet. "I didn't want Cherry Hill to miss the big game. And—well—the others thought I had put the skunk in the room. Porky said they would never believe the truth, because I'm not even an American—because I am a stranger here."

"So that was it," Miss Gray said slowly. "Domenic, Porky was very wrong. It is very wrong to lie. From now on, I must be able to trust you to tell the truth. And, you must trust me to believe it. That is the only way we can be real friends—not strangers. Will you promise me to do that?"

"I promise," Domenic said.

"Go along, then," said Miss Gray, smiling.

Domenic climbed over the stile. All the boys on the team were waiting for him. "Dom! Hey, Dommie," they called, as he climbed over the stile. Yes, they knew about Porky and the skunk, it was plain to see. The boys crowded around Domenic.

"I'm sure sorry about what happened," Will said. "You took an awful licking, just so we could win that game. We sure had you figured wrong, Dom."

"You were on our team all the way—only we didn't know it," Tim Jensen said.

"I *wish* I could be really on it!" Dom said shyly.

Will grinned. "I brought my ball and bat," he said. "We have time for a short game before the bell. Here, Dom, let's see you try a few pitches."

The boys walked out to the ball field. Dom looked down at the baseball he carried. It was only a little ball, dirty and worn. But Domenic felt as though he were holding the whole, wonderful world in his two hands.

LOOK-UP NAMES

LOOK-UP WORDS

BOOKS TO READ

LOOK-UP NAMES

Ah Gow *(ah gawh)*, a Chinese name.
Antonio *(ahn toh' nyoh)*, a Spanish or Italian first name meaning *Anthony*.
Ávila *(ah' ve lah)*, a Spanish last name.
Benito *(bay nee' toh)*, an Italian or Spanish first name meaning *Benedict*.
Bertoli *(bear toh' lee)*, an Italian last name.
Cabrillo *(kah bree' yoh)*, the last name of a Spanish explorer, the first white man to reach what is now California.
Californio *(cal' ee for' nee oh)*, a Spanish word meaning *Californian*, or a person from California.
Carlos *(kahr' lohs)*, a Spanish first name meaning *Charles*.
Carson River *(kahr' sun riv' ur)*, a river in the Sierra Nevada, running from California into Nevada.
Chumash *(choo' mash)*, a tribe of California Indians who lived near the ocean in southern California.
Dina *(dee' nah)*, an Italian first name.
Domenic *(doh' men ik)*, an Italian first name.
Fermín *(fayr meen')*, a Spanish first name.
Hop Wo Company *(hop woh kum' pah nih)*, the name of a Chinese company, or organization, that looked after and protected its members.
Independence *(in' de pen' dens)*, a town in Missouri, from which many pioneers started westward.
Inez *(eye' nez* or *ee' nez)*, a Spanish first name meaning *Agnes*.
José *(hoh say')*, a Spanish first name meaning *Joseph*.
Josefa *(hoh see' fah)*, a Spanish first name meaning *Josephine*.

183

Juan *(hwahn)*, a Spanish first name meaning *John*.
Kolok *(koh' lawk)*, the name of an Indian village.
La Paz *(lah pahz)*, a harbor and town on the southeastern coast of Lower California.
Loreto *(loh ray' toh)*, a town in Lower California.
Luisa *(loo ee' sah)*, a Spanish first name meaning *Louise* or *Louisa*.
Ma Chu *(mah chew)*, the Chinese goddess who protects sailors.
María *(mah ree' ah)*, a Spanish first name meaning *Marie, Maria,* or *Mary*.
Monterey *(mahn' te ray')*, the capital of California under Spanish rule.
Nimalala *(nee' mah lah' lah)*, the name of an Indian village.
Pió *(pee' oh)*, a Spanish first name.
Ramón *(ray mohn')*, a Spanish first name meaning *Raymond*.
Rosario *(roh sah' ree oh)*, a Spanish first name.
Sacramento *(sak' rah men' toh)*, a city in northern California that has been the capital of the state since 1854.
Salazar *(sa lah zahr')*, a Spanish first name.
Shuku *(shoo' koo)*, the name of an Indian village.
Sierra Nevada *(sih er' ah ne vah' dah)*, a long range of high mountains running from northwest to southeast along most of the eastern border of California.
Solá *(soh lah')*, a Spanish last name.
Sonora *(soh noh' rah)*, a part of Mexico along the Gulf of California.
Sutter's Fort *(sut' urz fort)*, a fort built by John Sutter in what is now Sacramento, the capital of California.
Teresa *(tah ray' sah)*, a Spanish first name meaning *Theresa*.
Tomás *(toh mahs')*, a Spanish first name meaning *Thomas*.
Tukan *(too' kan)*, the name of an Indian village.
Yat Sang *(yut sung)*, a Chinese man's or boy's name.

LOOK-UP WORDS

abalone *(ab' ah loh' ne)*, an ocean animal that lives in a shell.
adobe *(ah doh' bih)*, clay or some other kind of sticky earth from which bricks are made; also the sun-baked bricks made from such earth.
adventurer *(ad ven' chur ur)*, someone who looks for exciting experiences.
agent *(ay' jent)*, a person or company that acts for another.
altar *(awl' tur)*, a table or raised place in the most sacred part of a church; also a place on which sacrifices or offerings are made to a god or gods.
angleworm *(ang' gul wurm')*, an earthworm.
arbor *(ahr' bur)*, a frame over which vines or other twining plants are grown; also a place under such a vine-covered frame.

bamboo *(bam boo')*, a treelike grass with tall, stiff, hollow stems; also the stems of this plant.
banjo *(ban' joh)*, a stringed musical instrument played with the fingers.
bellows *(bel' ohz)*, a closed, boxlike device whose sides can be spread apart, then brought back together.
blacksmith *(blak' smith')*, a workman who shoes horses and shapes iron by heating it in a furnace, then hammering it into shape on an iron block, or anvil.
bolt *(bohlt)*, a roll or package, as a bolt of cloth.
bowie knife *(boh' ih* or *boo' ih nyf)*, a knife that has a long, **strong, single-edged blade.**

185

buckskin *(buk′ skin)*, leather made from the skin of a deer.
buenos dias *(bway′ nohs dee′ ahs)*, Spanish words meaning good day.
butter churn *(but′ ur churn)*, a wooden container in which butter is made from cream by beating and stirring.

calico *(kal′ ih koh)*, a kind of cotton cloth.
corral *(kah ral′ or ko rahl′)* a fenced-in place for cattle, horses, and other tame animals.
custom *(kus′ tum)*, the usual way of doing things; a way of life.

diggings *(dig′ ingz)*, any place where miners dig for gold or other minerals.
Don *(dahn)*, a Spanish title for an important man, meaning *Mr.* or *Sir.*
Doña *(doh′ nyah)*, a Spanish title for an important married woman, meaning *Mrs.* or *Lady.*
Dutch oven *(duch uv′ en)*, a covered iron kettle used for baking and roasting.

explorer *(eks plohr′ ur)*, one who travels into places about which little or nothing is known and tries to find out about them.

faith *(fayth)*, religion.
fare *(fair)*, the money a person pays to ride on a train, bus, ship, airplane, etc.
festival *(fes′ tih val)*, celebration of a special day or occasion; a holiday.
fire stick *(fyr stik)*, a stick used to make fire by rubbing it against another stick or another piece of wood.
flatiron *(flat′ eye′ urn)*, an iron used to iron clothes.

flint *(flint)*, a very hard rock, which Indians rubbed against a piece of metal to start a fire.
fork *(fork)*, a branch of a stream; the point at which a stream branches.

ginger *(jin' jur)*, a plant whose root is eaten or is used as a spice.
gong *(gawng)*, a kind of bell.
greens *(greenz)*, leaves and branches used for decoration.
guitar *(gih tahr')*, a stringed musical instrument, especially popular among Spaniards.

hacienda *(ah syen' dah* or *hah' sih en' dah)*, in Spanish American countries, a large estate or ranch on which farming, the raising of animals, and other kinds of work are done. Most of the workers live on the hacienda, which is usually a small community, with its own church, school, storehouses, and so on.
hardtack *(hahrd' tak')*, a kind of hard biscuit.
harpoon *(hahr poon')*, a long spear used in killing whales and other animals.
herb *(urb* or *hurb)*, a plant used as a food seasoning or a medicine.
homespun *(hohm' spun')*, cloth made at home or made of yarn spun at home.

industry *(in' dus trih)*, a business or trade, as the steel industry.

joss house *(jahs hous)*, a Chinese place of prayer. See *punk stick*.
junk *(jungk)*, a Chinese sailboat.

lean-to *(leen' too')*, a small building or shelter having a single-pitched roof and leaning against a rock, a tree, or another building.

legend *(lej' end)*, a tale that has come down from the past.

lichee *(lee' che)*, a small, nut-shaped Oriental fruit, which is often dried and eaten.

livery stable *(liv' ur ih stay' bul)*, a place where horses and horse-drawn vehicles are kept.

Long Tom *(lawng tahm)*, a washing trough used to separate gold from dirt and sand.

loom *(loom)*, a machine used for weaving cloth.

lye water *(ly waht' ur)*, a liquid made by slowly dissolving wood ashes. It was used in early days in making soap.

mainland *(mayn' land')*, a large body of land, as a continent.

mane *(mayn)*, the heavy hair that grows on the neck of a horse.

mare *(mair)*, a female horse.

matanza *(mah tahn' sah)*, the Spanish name for a slaughtering or a large-scale killing of animals.

metate *(may tah' tay)*, the Spanish name of a hollowed-out stone used in grinding seeds and grains.

miracle *(mir' ah kul)*, something so unusual that it cannot be explained as a natural happening; a marvel.

moon *(moon)*, a month, or the time which the moon takes to revolve about the earth.

muslin *(muz' lin)*, a kind of cotton cloth.

muy bonita *(moo' eh bo nee' tah)*, Spanish words meaning *very pretty*.

nose bag *(nohz bag)*, a feed bag that covers an animal's nose and is fastened over the top of its head. The bag is filled with grain or other feed for the animal.

padrone *(pah droh' nay)*, an Italian word meaning *landlord* or *landowner*.

pass *(pass)*, a narrow passage through mountains.

pasta *(pahs' tah)*, an Italian word meaning *paste,* such as macaroni, spaghetti, etc.

patio *(pah' tih oh* or *pah' tyoh)*, the Spanish name for an inside courtyard of a house, which is open to the sky.

pay dirt *(pay durt)*, dirt that contains gold or some other valuable mineral.

peasant *(pez' ant)*, a poor countryman, often a man who works as a farm laborer.

plain *(playn)*, a stretch of flat land.

pueblo *(pweb' loh)*, a Spanish word meaning *town*.

pulley *(pull' ih)*, a small, rimmed wheel used with a rope, chain, wire, or belt to make the raising and lowering of heavy things easier.

punk stick *(pungk stik)*, a stick covered with a special kind of hardened paste; it is burned in joss houses as an offering. See *joss house*.

queue *(kyoo)*, a braid of hair hanging down behind one's head. At one time, most Chinese men wore queues.

rancheria *(rahn chay ree' ah)*, a Spanish word meaning *village*.

ranchero *(rahn chay' roh)*, a Spanish word meaning *rancher* or *farmer*.

rancho *(rahn' choh)*, a Spanish word meaning a *ranch* or a *farm* where cattle or other tame animals are raised.

sacred *(say' kred)*, religious; holy.

salami *(sah lah' me)*, a kind of sausage which is smoked or dried and is popular among Italians.

salt pork *(sawlt pohrk)*, pork cured in salt or in a salty liquid to make it keep a long time.

sassafras *(sas' ah fras)*, a kind of tree whose bark and leaves are used for medicine or flavoring.

sawhorse *(saw' hors')*, a kind of wooden frame on which wood is put to be sawed.

scurvy *(skur' vih)*, a sickness causing weakness; bad breath; spongy, bleeding gums; loosening teeth; and so on. It results from a lack of vitamin C, often from not eating enough fresh vegetables and fruits.

señor *(say nyor')*, a Spanish word meaning *Mr.* or *sir*.

señora *(say nyoh' rah)*, a Spanish word meaning *Mrs.* or *madam*.

sí *(see)*, a Spanish word meaning *yes*.

smallpox *(smawl' pahks')*, a contagious disease.

stake a claim *(stayk a klaym)*, to mark off the limits of a piece of property by sticks or posts.

stern *(sturn)*, strict; severe.

stile *(styl)*, steps built for use in getting over a fence or wall.

sweat house *(swet hous)*, a kind of bathhouse and a gathering place where the men of some Indian tribes met to talk, smoke, and sleep.

tallow *(tal' oh)*, the melted fat of cattle or sheep. It is used in making such things as soap and candles.

tongue *(tung)*, a language.

tortilla *(tor tee' yah)*, a thin, flat, round cake made from ground corn.

vaquero *(vah kay' roh)*, a Spanish word for *cowboy*.

Yankee *(yang' ke)*, a person from one of the New England states; a nickname for any native of the United States.

BOOKS TO READ

ADAMS, SAMUEL HOPKINS. *The Pony Express.* Random, 1950. This is a story of brave riders and lonely trails, and of three men who fought to bring fast mail to the Far West.

ALDERMAN, FRANCES L., and WILSON, AMBER M. *About Los Angeles.* Heath, 1948. This book tells the story of Los Angeles—from Spanish pueblo to present-day metropolis.

BLACKBURN, EDITH H. *The Bells of Carmel.* Aladdin, 1954. Aptos, an Indian boy, finds adventure and friendship with Father Junípero Serra at the mission in Carmel.

BUELL, ROBERT KINGERY. *California Stepping-Stones.* Stanford, 1948. This book is a history of California for boys and girls.

BULLA, CLYDE ROBERT. *Riding the Pony Express.* Crowell, 1948. Owl Creek Station burns to the ground, and young Dick Park must see that the mail goes through.

COSTANTINO, JOAN and JOSEPHINE. *Pepito at Capistrano.* Whitman, 1943. Pepito, an Indian boy, celebrates his birthday on March 19th—the day on which legend says the swallows return to Capistrano Mission each year.

DEL REY, LESTER. *A Pirate Flag for Monterey.* Winston, 1952. A fire at sea, a stormy night in a lifeboat, a battle with pirates, and a city in flames—these were the adventures Mike found in the California of another day.

EVERNDEN, MARGERY. *The Golden Trail.* Random, 1952. With his family, Ramón follows the Anza Trail from Mexico to New California.

Garthwaite, Marion. *Tomás and the Red Headed Angel.* Messner, 1950. An Indian boy and a Spanish girl help each other to find freedom from a cruel master in this tale of rancho days.

Heffernan, Helen, et al. *Desert Treasure.* Wagner, 1955. This fast-paced "western" mystery tells about the adventures of two boys as they search for a lost gold mine and track down an outlaw gang in the Mojave Desert.

Lewis, Oscar. *The Story of California.* Garden City, 1955. This book tells the history of our state.

McNeer, May. *The California Gold Rush.* Random, 1950. This is a thrilling story of the discovery of gold near Sutter's Fort in 1848 and of the rush to California that followed.

Merrell, Leigh. *Tenoch.* Nelson, 1954. Tenoch, the son of a Spanish conquistador and an Indian mother, sails as a cabin boy with Juan Rodríguez Cabrillo to the coast of California.

Nathan, Adele. *The Building of the First Transcontinental Railroad.* Random, 1950. A trail of wood and steel joins the far ends of our nation.

Politi, Leo. *Song of the Swallows.* Scribner, 1949. A young boy at the Capistrano Mission waits for spring and his friends' return.

Robinson, W. W. *Beasts of the Tar Pits.* Ritchie, 1949. This book tells of the strange beasts that roamed California before the coming of man.

Stewart, George R. *To California by Covered Wagon.* Random, 1954. A true story of the Stevens party, who came overland to California in 1844.

Tousey, Sanford. *Jerry and the Pony Express.* Doubleday, 1954. Jerry and his horse, Buster, find a way to help a brave Pony Express rider.